Ideology and Interpellation

Also Available from Bloomsbury

The Real is Radical, Jonathan Fardy
Art, Politics and Rancière, Tina Chanter
Egalitarian Moments: From Descartes to Rancière, Devin Zane Shaw
Encountering Althusser: Politics and Materialism in Contemporary Radical Thought, Katja Diefenbach

Ideology and Interpellation

Anti-humanism to Non-philosophy

Jonathan Fardy

BLOOMSBURY ACADEMIC
LONDON • NEW YORK • OXFORD • NEW DELHI • SYDNEY

BLOOMSBURY ACADEMIC
Bloomsbury Publishing Plc, 50 Bedford Square, London, WC1B 3DP, UK
Bloomsbury Publishing Inc, 1385 Broadway, New York, NY 10018, USA
Bloomsbury Publishing Ireland, 29 Earlsfort Terrace, Dublin 2, D02 AY28, Ireland

BLOOMSBURY, BLOOMSBURY ACADEMIC and the Diana logo
are trademarks of Bloomsbury Publishing Plc

First published in Great Britain 2024
This paperback edition published 2025

Copyright © Jonathan Fardy, 2024

Jonathan Fardy has asserted his right under the Copyright, Designs and Patents Act, 1988, to be identified as Author of this work.

For legal purposes the Acknowledgments on p. vi constitute an extension of this copyright page.

Series design by Charlotte Daniels
Cover image: Philippe Gras / Le Pictorium – May 68 – 1968 – France / Ile-de-France (region) / Paris – The damage following the various demonstrations in the streets (© Philippe Gras / Alamy Stock Photo)

All rights reserved. No part of this publication may be: i) reproduced or transmitted in any form, electronic or mechanical, including photocopying, recording or by means of any information storage or retrieval system without prior permission in writing from the publishers; or ii) used or reproduced in any way for the training, development or operation of artificial intelligence (AI) technologies, including generative AI technologies. The rights holders expressly reserve this publication from the text and data mining exception as per Article 4(3) of the Digital Single Market Directive (EU) 2019/790.

Bloomsbury Publishing Inc does not have any control over, or responsibility for, any third-party websites referred to or in this book. All internet addresses given in this book were correct at the time of going to press. The author and publisher regret any inconvenience caused if addresses have changed or sites have ceased to exist, but can accept no responsibility for any such changes.

A catalogue record for this book is available from the British Library.

A catalog record for this book is available from the Library of Congress.

ISBN: HB: 978-1-3503-5891-1
PB: 978-1-3503-5895-9
ePDF: 978-1-3503-5892-8
eBook: 978-1-3503-5893-5

Typeset by Integra Software Services Pvt. Ltd.

For product safety related questions contact productsafety@bloomsbury.com.

To find out more about our authors and books visit www.bloomsbury.com and sign up for our newsletters.

Contents

Acknowledgments   vi

1   Introduction   1
2   Althusser (Part I)   7
3   Althusser (Part II)   27
4   Rancière   63
5   Baudrillard   93
6   Laruelle   119
7   Conclusion   149

Bibliography   154
Index   160

Acknowledgments

This book would not have been possible without all the students I have had the honor and pleasure to teach. I dedicate this to them.

1

Introduction

I had initially envisioned a book about the "legacy" of Louis Althusser's concept of ideological "interpellation" as reflected in the work of Jacques Rancière, Jean Baudrillard, and François Laruelle. No doubt each of these thinkers responded to concepts, orientations, and positions in Althusser's work. But the lines of filiation traverse the spectrum from rejection (Rancière), subversion (Baudrillard), and radicalization (Laruelle). However, all of these thinkers are linked by a concern to conceptualize the constitution of the subject by forms of address that operationalize subjectification: by state power (Althusser), by the intellectual class (Rancière), by the simulacral object (Baudrillard), and by philosophy itself (Laruelle).

It is not my contention that these thinkers can be seamlessly combined into a coherent theory of ideology. Quite to the contrary. A comparative reading reveals in sharp detail how incomparable these figures are. My aim is different. A comparative reading enables us to grasp the contours of a problematic that any contemporary theory of ideology must confront. How should ideology be conceptually framed after the *deconstruction of the subject* and how must critique be reimagined in order to do that? The humanist subject has indeed withered under various (post)structuralist critiques. But this very process of critique has itself taken the form of a *subject of knowledge* seemingly equipped with sufficient reason to see beyond the ideology of the human. This promotion of theory's power makes theory itself operatively a kind of stand-in for the humanist subject of old. Granted this subject-position of theory is not the same as the humanist subject. But it raises a thorny question that these chapters attempt to deal with: what is the role of theory? What is this subject position? How does it account for its own conditions of possibility? How to account for, in the words of Homi Bhabha, the "tensions and ambivalences that mark this enigmatic place from which theory speaks."[1] Theory for Althusser, Rancière, Baudrillard, and Laruelle always speaks from a-subjective standpoint: the standpoint of science (Althusser), of history (Rancière), of the object (Baudrillard), and of non-philosophy in the name of the human beyond humanism (Laruelle). The following chapters can be read then independently. Althusser, Rancière, Baudrillard, and Laruelle have, in ways unique to their projects, attempted to renew the possibility of ideological critique without defaulting into uncritical humanism. The way each went about this differed greatly from one another. But the projects spring from a common concern to dissolve the traditional linkage of ideology to that of "false consciousness."

My selection of thinkers is by no means entirely an obvious selection. Rancière studied under Althusser and contributed to *Reading Capital*. But he unequivocally rejected the teaching of his teacher in 1974. His break with Althusserianism, however, illuminates its pedagogical dimension and opens to view the entire problem of the interpellative power of the intellectual class over the political subjects it aims to recruit. Baudrillard might appear at first glance quite outside the Althusserian legacy. But his prioritization of the *object over the subject* opens a path for a renewed practice of ideological critique after the deconstruction of the subject. His work models a form of theory that attempts to grasp the material, or *objectal*, conditions of the simulacrum. He answers the hailing or interpellative power of the simulacrum by insisting on treating it as an object and not as referential lure. Finally, Laruelle offers a means to consider the *ideology of philosophy* and offers indications for how to liberate philosophical materials from the ideological closure imposed by standard philosophy.

A thread that I follow through the chapters is the materiality of theoretical inscription. The question of the very possibility of a theory of ideology requires an interrogation of the theoretical, political, and even aesthetic dimension of theoretical work. This constellation of concerns orbits around a seemingly traditional doublet: subject and object. The *question of the subject* is a core problem for all four thinkers. Althusser's theory of ideology is a theory of what it means to be always-already hailed as a subject. Rancière's post-Althusserian historiographic work is a theory of how to learn from "empirical proletarians" who refused the interpellative call: *to work*. Baudrillard's objectal theory is haunted by the disappearance of the subject from the horizon of the object. Laruelle's nonstandard philosophy critiques standard philosophy as a form of epistemological subjection. This constellation opens a complex three-pronged problematic: that of the subject, the subject of theory, and the theory of ideology as that of the subject.

Outline of Chapters

Chapter 2 examines the prehistory of Althusser's theory of ideology. It focuses on his "theoreticist" period marked by the publication in 1965 of *Reading Capital* and *For Marx*. I trace Althusser's anti-humanist epistemology through Jean Cavaillès and others who affirmed the necessity of a *philosophy of the concept* (as against philosophies of consciousness). I argue that Althusser ultimately situates "theory" itself as an agent of transformation. "Theory" takes the place of the subject (or displaces the place of the subject) in order to beat back the political forces of liberalism then on the rise in the post-Stalinist reformism of actually existing Communist parties.

Chapter 3 examines Althusser's 1970 essay "Ideology and Ideological State Apparatuses" (ISAs essay) in the context of French

Maoism then on the march. Thus, we move from Chapter 2's focus on "the subject of theory" to Chapter 3's focus on the "theory of the subject." The chapter concludes with a reading of the ISAs essay.

Chapter 4 examines the early work of Rancière, starting with his break with Althusser enunciated in *Althusser's Lesson*, published in 1974. Disappointed with Althusser's reluctance to accord May 1968 theoretical or political significance, Rancière turned his back on Althusserianism *and on all theoretical orientations that do not begin with the thought immanent to resistance enacted by dominated peoples*. He turned to the archives to carry out a historiographic intervention on the subject of past revolts. I focus primarily on *Proletarian Nights*, Rancière's study of nineteenth-century French workers. Rancière's study is constructed around a set of select case studies of declassed subjects and precarious workers who dreamed of another form of work: that of aesthetic and philosophical production. Rancière's text puts considerable pressure on the Althusserian concept of ideology in that Rancière's case studies are workers who did not identify with work. They did not heed the interpellative call or hail: *to work.* Neither did they heed the interpellative call of the proto-socialist intellectual formations that hailed them also as workers. Their oneiric resistance signaled a politically acute resistance to work itself. At the very moment in which Rancière was finding political and intellectual resources untapped by Althusserianism, workers against work were on the march in Italy under the banners of Autonomy. The autonomous movements of Italy and the historiographic work of Rancière suggest the possibility of subjectivation constituted through a radical refusal of the interpellative solicitation.

Chapter 5 looks at the work of Baudrillard. My concern is to surface the objectal dimension of his later (post-1975) work. Baudrillard displaces the question of the subject by a theoretical prioritization of the simulacral *object*. Baudrillard demystifies the simulacrum by treating it as an object of theory. I situate Baudrillard's work in light of Gregory Ulmer's pathbreaking concept of "post-criticism," which refuses the mimeticism of traditional criticism. Post-critical theory does not refer directly to an object outside its conceptual matrix. But I argue that Baudrillard's objectal form of critique is haunted by the subject that it dispels. From the vantage point of Baudrillard's haunted objectal theoretical form, one can reread Althusser's theory of ideology as the theory of an object—that of the ISAs—as likewise haunted by the question of the subject.

Finally, Chapter 6 examines the nonstandard philosophy of Laruelle. I conclude with Laruelle because his approach complements, but radically extends, the concerns of the prior three thinkers. His work, like Rancière's, refuses the lure of philosophy *qua* master discourse sufficient to determine or decide another discourse or practice. It refuses then the form (if not the content) of anything like *philosophy of politics, philosophy of art, philosophy of language*, etc. And that also means that Laruelle rejects in principle the very idea of a *philosophy (or theory) of ideology*. I deploy Laruelle's concepts in order to surface the aesthetic investments in the ISAs essay. My interests (via Laruelle) lie in the ISAs essay's implied photographic logic. Following Laruelle, I ask: how does a certain *photographism* in the essay underwrite what Paul de Man might have identified as the essay's "aesthetic ideology"?

This book finally aims to show what the stakes and demands are for any theory of ideology that dispenses with the humanist subject and its cognate concepts—consciousness above all else—and to show how those stakes and demands can be brought into sharper focus by this constellation of thinkers.

Note

1 Homi K. Bhabha, *The Location of Culture* (London: Routledge, 1994), 33.

2

Althusser (Part I)

Science of Ideas

Georges Labica reminds us that the term *ideology* was coined by the eighteenth-century French philosopher and political economist, Destutt de Tracy. It meant for him "science of ideas." An aristocrat by birth, de Tracy became an enlightenment philosopher and revolutionary sympathizer. De Tracy's *Elements of Ideology* of 1796 sought to establish a "supplement of physiology."[1] Ideology was to be a science of the body of ideas as physiology is a science of the physical body. His aim was, he wrote, to "acquaint the reader in detail with what takes place in himself when he thinks, speaks, and reasons."[2] For de Tracy, "ideology" was to replace philosophy. But already in his lifetime "ideology" took on a pejorative connotation. De Tracy and his followers were denounced as "ideologues:" those who peddle falsehoods and mystifications. Marx followed suit in his usage of the term. In *The German Ideology*, Marx and Engels denounce as "ideology" any form of thought that grants ideas independence of their material basis. Any philosophy that is blind to its material conditions of possibility—and presents ideas as independent (in the manner of de Tracy)—is on that score "ideology" in the bad sense. This sense is indexed in *The German Ideology*. Allow me to quote it at length:

> If in all ideology men and their relations appear upside-down as in a *camera obscura*, this phenomenon arises just as much from their historical life-process as the inversion of objects on the retina does from their physical life process. In direct contrast to German

philosophy which descends from heaven to earth, here it is a matter of ascending from earth to heaven. The phantoms formed in the brains of men are also, necessarily, sublimates of their material life-process, which is empirically verifiable and bound to material premises. Morality, religion, metaphysics, and all the rest of ideology as well as the forms of consciousness corresponding to these, thus no longer retain the semblance of independence.[3]

Ideology is any form of thought that does not recognize thought's immanent conditioning by material conditions. A science of ideas for Marx to be a true science can only be in the last instance a science of historical materialism. But in this first formulation, as Sarah Kofman has astutely noted, Marx and Engels do not give a materialist account of how it is that ideas can appear independent of the material conditions that constitute them. "Where, however, within ideology," asks Kofman, "comes the illusion of independence?"[4] What is left unspecified in *The German Ideology* is a materialist account of the relationship between material conditions and the semblance of free-floating ideas. This in part is the problem that Marx attempts to resolve in *Capital* with his concept of "commodity fetishism."

Concept vs. Consciousness

The history of Marxist theories of ideology is divided (at least) in two. One camp holds that ideology is an illusory form of consciousness. The other—to which Althusser belongs—holds that ideology is a material condition, one of the effects of which is precisely the very concept of "consciousness." The battle between the camps takes place on many fields. But one to which the battle returns again and again is the conceptual terrain demarcated by Marx's concept of commodity fetishism. Let us review. Marx writes:

> There is a physical relation between physical things. But it is different with commodities. There, the existence of things *qua*

commodities, and the value relation between the products of labor which stamps them as commodities, have absolutely no connection with their physical properties and with the material relations arising therefrom. There is a definite social relation between men, that assumes, in their eyes, the fantastic form of a relation between things. In order, therefore, to find an analogy, we must have recourse to the mist-enveloped regions of the religious world. ... This I call the Fetishism which attaches itself to the products of labor, so soon as they are produced as commodities, and which is therefore inseparable from the production of commodities.[5]

Georg Lukács based his theory of *reification* on commodity fetishism. Reification (literally meaning "thingafication") is a social process that leads to a form of consciousness by which persons come to regard one another as mere things of use. For example, workers are regarded as useful for the production of value from the standpoint of capitalism. Lukács's antidote is *proletarian consciousness* embodied in the Bolshevik Party form.

Althusser rejects the concept of reification. Ideology for him is not a problem of consciousness primarily. He regards Lukács's theory itself as symptomatic of liberal-bourgeois ideology. The concept of "consciousness" is inextricably bound up with the bourgeois political concept of possessive individualism. Nick Nesbitt extends this argument. Nesbitt notes that the problem is not that persons under capital regard one another as *useful things*. Rather, the problem is that persons regard one another as mere indices of *value*. Nesbitt writes:

> Marx's point [about commodity fetishism] is *not* that in capitalism people relate to one another as *useful things,* that, as Lukács argued, they "reify" one another (although this is surely the case as well); rather, Marx is literally saying that when the commodity is the predominant social form of relations, what appears and counts as valuable in any thing [or person] is not reified use value but its exchange value. ... In capitalism, as the saying goes, everyone and everything has its price.[6]

Persons come to regard one another as indices of value, however, not by *thinking* this in the first instance. This form of consciousness is an effect of the material conditions of value production. The "transference of human relations to relations between things," notes Alfred Sohn-Rethel, "in other words the 'reifying' property of exchange is bound up with the equating effect which the act of exchange exercises upon objects."[7] It is the *act* of exchange alone that "exercises" and effects the establishment of commodity fetishism and not the consciousness of those party to the exchange in the first instance. Althusser, like Sohn-Rethel, dismisses consciousness as a first cause of ideology. Althusser seeks a theory of ideology likewise rooted in material conditions and therefore amenable to scientific formalization. Where Althusser differs from Sohn-Rethel is that Althusser opts instead for a materialist theory of ideology rooted in the material workings of state apparatuses.

Militantly Conceptual

The *philosophy of the concept* names a line of thought opposed to philosophies of consciousness, the subject, and the human in the last instance.[8] Its twentieth-century roots lie in the work of Jean Cavaillès who coined the phrase "philosophy of the concept" in his last work, *On Logic and the Theory of Science*. This he wrote in a Nazi prison camp prior to his eventual execution by firing squad for his role in the French Resistance.

On Logic and the Theory of Science is a difficult text. Its condensed and elliptical form cedes little to the uninitiated. Cavaillès asserts that the history of mathematics requires acceptance of demonstrable truths not subject to historical change at the same time as it forces consideration of the historicity of mathematical invention. "Cavaillès believed that the history of mathematics posed special problems for philosophy," notes Knox Peden, "in that the truths articulated in this science were universal in their remit and yet the process of their discovery was temporal."⁹ Mathematical truths are produced in material history, but these truths are universal and not bound by the historicity of their production. In "logic or mathematics ... there is no readymade relationship to externality," explains Peden, "and yet a relation persists, between the logical or mathematical relations and the judgment of them *as logical or mathematical relations*."¹⁰

Cavaillès asserts that scientific truth emerges in "a conceptual becoming that cannot be halted."¹¹ Scientific experiment marks the advent of this emergent autonomy. Experiment for Cavaillès does not yield knowledge of the real. It is instead the forced isolation of phenomena and their radical parameterization by those rules. Experiment forecloses all but *the strict construction of the object of knowledge* determined by the apodictic rules of construction necessary for that object. "Far from being an involvement in nature," writes Cavaillès, "the experiment is, on the contrary, the incorporation of the world into the scientific universe."¹² The production of scientific knowledge for Cavaillès is the forced expulsion of nonexperimental exteriority. "Thus scientific autonomy is simultaneously expansion and closure," concludes Cavaillès, "a negative closure in its refusal to take input from, or end up arriving back at, the outside world."¹³ Here we can detect the operation of the crucial Spinozist distinction that will be fundamental to Althusser's theoretical work: *the object of knowledge is distinct from the real object.*

As Peden shows in his landmark book, *Spinoza Contra Phenomenology*, Cavaillès gave renewed vigor to the tradition of French rationalism that defined the rules of engagement for Althusser and his circle. Cavaillès's example also tenuously suggested a relation between scientific and political practice. Cavaillès's participation in the Resistance lent his extraordinarily abstract work an air of Left political militancy. Cavaillès's remarkable commitment to thought— the fact that he wrote up *On Logic and the Theory of Science* in a Nazi prison camp—gave Althusser's generation a model to follow. They too steadfastly committed themselves to rigorously theoretical, logical, and scientific thought, but this time in the name of politics itself.

Georges Canguilhem, Gaston Bachelard, and Charles Ehresmann played a decisive role in the preservation and dissemination of Cavaillès's work. Bachelard and Ehresmann edited and titled Cavaillès's manuscript and wrote the introduction for the 1946 edition. There they argue that Cavaillès's political and philosophical works were intimately linked. They write:

[Cavaillès] became one of the four or five founders of the Resistance movements in France. The extent of Cavaillès's work in this domain, up until his second and final arrest in August 1943, was staggering. Yet he did not allow this task to distract him from his philosophical work. Indeed, for him the two could not really be separated. He considered it entirely necessary to return to philosophical reflection in the midst of action, so as to preserve his sanity.[14]

Perhaps it was simply a case of mental survival. But it could be interpreted with equal justice as a political act. Cavaillès along with intellectuals such as Simone Weil and Raymond Aron considered philosophical and political commitment of equal importance. Aron reported that Cavaillès had declared on one occasion: "I'm a Spinozist ... we must resist, fight, and confront death. Truth and reason demand it."[15] But, as Peden points out, Aron recounted this statement slightly differently in a commemoration for Cavaillès at the Sorbonne in 1945. On that occasion, he noted that Cavaillès had said: "I'm a Spinozist; I believe we submit to the necessary everywhere. The sequences of mathematicians are necessary; even the [historical] stages of mathematical science are necessary. This struggle that we carry out is necessary as well."[16] Whatever the exact wording, it appears that Cavaillès held that mathematical logic and political resistance were immanent to a greater logic of necessity as such.

Cavaillès's logico-political commitment galvanized an entire generation of French intellectuals. "Indeed, Cavaillès has been a touchstone for radical French thinkers," notes Peden, "from Althusser to Foucault to Badiou."[17] Peden continues:

> In each instance, there is the intimation of a link between Cavaillès's philosophy, which, to be clear, was in no way a political theory, and his manifest heroism in the face of death. ... At best there is an allusive equivocation between Nazi forces of Occupation and the contemporary enemies of the political left. In other words, Cavaillès's Spinozist commitment to necessity merely gives the form of Resistance and the contours of tenacity. Yet, because Cavaillès was philosophically opposed to philosophies of consciousness, it is as if one might perform a logical deduction that then establishes the political superiority of a philosophy of the concept to the proliferation of meaning that followed upon the arrival of phenomenology in France.[18]

Cavaillès's example set the groundwork for Althusser and his circle's commitment to "theoretical formation" in the 1960s. Their commitment to a scientific reading of Marx (and Marxism) was a commitment to its theoretical formalization against all philosophies of consciousness, including humanism, historicism, phenomenology, and empiricism. They saw their task as liberating scientific Marxism from the "occupation" of thought by philosophies of consciousness and all forms of subject-centric philosophy, which they denounced as enemy forces in service to ideology.

Politics of Theoretical Formation

Althusser's students took theoretical formation as a political necessity. Their turn to theory was also an act of defiance against the Marxist-humanist dogmatism of the French Communist Party (PCF). This became the official philosophy of Communist parties at the Twentieth Congress of the Communist Party of the Soviet Union (CPSU).[19]

Nikita Khrushchev's denunciation of Stalinism aggravated and exacerbated the already growing Sino-Soviet split. Mao Zedong declared the CPSU "revisionist." Mao's admirers among Althusser's circle followed suit. They turned to theory as means to carry out a political corrective to revisionism. Mao's writings appeared to authorize this turn to theory. He declared in 1957 that correct theory was a political necessity. Mao writes in "On the Correct Handling of Contradictions among the People":

> Intellectuals ... should not be complacent. They must continue to remold themselves, gradually shed their bourgeois world outlook and acquire the proletarian, communist outlook so they can fully fit in with the needs of the new society and unite with the workers and peasants. ... We hope that they [intellectuals] will continue to make progress and that, in the course of work and study, they will gradually acquire the communist world outlook, get a better grasp of Marxism-Leninism and become integrated with the workers and peasants.[20]

Mao affirms Lenin's conviction that revolutionary practice requires revolutionary theory.

Althusser and his circle saw it as their political duty to produce adequate concepts needed to restore the revolutionary orientation of Communist politics. Theoretical work was now seen as politically indispensable. "Indispensable theoretical concepts do not magically construct themselves on command when they are needed," writes Althusser in *Reading Capital*, the "whole history of the beginnings of sciences or of great philosophies shows, on the contrary, that the exact set of new concepts do not march out on parade in single file; on the contrary some are long delayed, or march in borrowed clothes before acquiring their proper uniforms."[21] Here are encapsulated two central ideas for Althusser: theory is concept production and concepts can be "symptomatically" produced in an outmoded language foreign or even antithetical to the logic of the science they operationalize. For Althusser, the latter is the case with the Young Marx's humanism. Althusser's rhetoric is also clearly that of a militant. Concepts have to be properly uniformed, outfitted, disciplined, and deployed. None of this happens by magic. It happens by disciplined training.

Althusser's insistence on the political necessity of theoretical training set the tone for the constitution of an important journal to which many of his students would contribute: *Cahiers pour l'Analyse*. The journal reflected Althusser's teaching that theoretical training was vital for political practice. As Peter Hallward notes with reference to Althusser's 1963 essay "Theory, Theoretical Training, and Theoretical Formation":

> The most urgent priority, as Althusser had repeatedly insisted, was the theoretical training ... of a new revolutionary generation, one whose grasp of Marxist science would reverse the disastrous revisionist steps taken by the older generation and return the [French Communist] Party to its proper course. The goal should be to "extend the broadest possible *theoretical training* to the greatest possible number of militants," "to educate then constantly in theory, to make them militants in the full sense of the term" in other words "militants capable of one day becoming men and women of science." ... Only appropriate theoretical training and the importation of Marxist science can guard against the expression of ideological or spontaneous i.e. untrained reflexes (veering from utopian-anarchist to chastened-reformist) among students and workers alike.[22]

It is hard perhaps to imagine the political urgency that "high theory" had for Althusser's students. That generation is popularly identified with the events of May 1968 and its cry: *back to practice*. But many of Althusser's students actually opposed (at least early on) the events of May on the grounds that it represented a "spontaneous" or "ideological" rebellion rather than a scientific-strategic revolution. Cool theoretical detachment reflected the students' zealous discipline, a militantly conceptual commitment, for which Cavaillès again served as a model.

Reflecting in an interview on his involvement with *Cahiers pour l'Analyse*, Yves Duroux notes: "There is someone ... who needs to be mentioned: Jean Cavaillès. It was the moment when people began to talk about him, and following his example, to take more of an interest in modern mathematics."[23] Cavaillès set an example by his sartorially steadfast pursuit of science in the face of fascist terror. If Cavaillès was capable of persevering in his pursuit of science from within the confines of a Nazi prison, then, so they thought, should they be able to resist the siren call of action for the painstaking labor needed for the scientific rectification of Marxist theory.

Philosophies of consciousness and the subject were to be dispatched in search of the structuring processes for which "consciousness" and "subject" were ideologically structured effects.

The dialectic between structuring forces and structured results was a key methodological motif of *Cahiers pour l'Analyse*. Duroux clarifies this point in reference to Althusser's formulation: history is a *process without a subject*. It "is a process without a subject," notes Duroux, "in the sense that the action of the structure is not itself the action of a subject" but this meant for students, like Duroux, that it was necessary to "reintroduce the subject" so as "to have the duality of the structuring and the structured."[24] It is easy to think of Althusserian theory as simply a critique of the subject. Althusser's well-known formula—*history is a process without a subject*—certainly lends credence to this view. But the formula's nuance becomes apparent in light of the central methodological motif of *Cahiers pour l'Analyse*: the structuring-structured relationship. History is indeed a *process without a subject*, but historical processes do produce subjects *and* theories of subjects. We can trace a line of connection between Althusser and Sohn-Rethel on this point. Sohn-Rethel argues that there is no subject of the exchange abstraction prior to the processual act of exchange. The process of exchange structures the relation between the agents as *subjects of exchange*. Likewise, for Althusser, there are no subjects prior to the social, historical, political processes that produce them. For Althusser and Sohn-Rethel, these processes are "real abstractions" that produce their subjects.

Concept Production

Althusser and his students set their sights by Bachelard's watchword, which served as the epigraph to each issue of *Cahiers pour l'Analyse*: "work a concept."[25] They collectively affirmed a materialist theory of knowledge for which the concept has to be produced. Knowledge of capital could not in their view be gleaned from empirical data. This was Marx's lesson.

The empiricist process of knowledge acquisition holds that the real contains knowledge. "The whole empiricist conception of knowledge," writes Althusser in *Reading Capital*, "lies in fact in an operation of the subject called *abstraction*."[26] The empiricist approach assumes that the subject *qua* knower abstracts or extracts knowledge from the empirically real. "For the empiricist conception of knowledge, the whole of knowledge is thus invested *in the real*," writes Althusser, "and knowledge never arises except as *a relation inside its real object between the really distinct parts of that real object.*"[27]

The empiricist conception of knowledge necessarily commits itself to a nonempirical postulate. It holds that real objects (parts of empirical reality) contain knowledge as if, for example, the hydrogen atom contains the equations of quantum physics. "*This investment of knowledge, conceived as a real part of the real object, in the real structure of the real object,*" writes Althusser, "*is what constitutes the specific problematic of the empiricist conception of knowledge.*"[28] The empiricist conception of knowledge also problematically presumes that there are already clearly defined "subjects" and "objects." In the empiricist conception of knowledge, "the subject and object ... are given," notes Althusser, "and hence predate the process of knowledge."[29] For Althusser and his students, the place and relation of subject and object are not "given" but are produced by a "certain fundamental theoretical field, but one which cannot ... be pronounced *empiricist.*"[30] It cannot be "pronounced *empiricist,*" according to Althusser, because "subject" and "object" are not empirical entities but concepts derived from the "theoretical field" of post-Kantian bourgeois philosophy. Subject and object are not mere "givens" but conceptual products structured by certain implicit or explicit theoretical commitments. The subject-object schema is thus not a starting point for inquiry but a result of structuring processes which require interrogation and theorization.

Cadre Production

Althusser and his circle had a fraught and at times openly hostile relationship with the PCF. Indeed, one of the chief reasons why Althusser embarked on his "return to Marx" was to check the PCF's embrace of Moscow's Marxist-humanist line. Relations between Althusser and his students were at times equally fraught with some feeling that their political role had been curtailed by their teacher's demand to study and theoretically prepare. Althusser defended his stance on the grounds that autonomy in theoretical practice was necessary for the development of Marxist science. This Althusser stresses in the essay "Student Problems" published in 1964.

Althusser argues that the liberal university at its best should function as an independent sphere of intellectual action. The autonomy of the liberal university secures the autonomy of science and enables its free development. The goal of Communist students should be, notes Althusser, "to discover new scientific knowledge capable of illuminating and criticizing the overwhelming ideological illusions in which *everyone is imprisoned*."[31]

Despite Althusser's criticism of the PCF, he remained a loyal member. He was in this narrow sense a *party theorist* who saw it as his duty to supply the PCF with scientific theory, dispel ideology, and produce future party cadre. Gregory Elliott explains Althusser's position in "Student Problems" as such:

> Since the "revolutionary cause" is founded on science, Communist students should prioritize the demarcation of science from ideology—the defense and promotion of the former against the latter. As regards Marxist science, they were under two obligations: its "assimilation" and "dissemination, defense, and illustration." ... Althusser concluded ... by reminding Communist students of their responsibility to "aid the party" in its struggles.[32]

Althusser argues that students should steel themselves for the hard labor of theoretical production in service to the party's founding revolutionary aim. But only if Marxist science is free to develop autonomously can theorists supply the knowledge needed for the party to fulfill its historical mission. The link between theory (concept production) and political commitment (cadre production) left open a difficult question. What is it that produces concepts and thereby political effects? What (or who) is the subject of theory?

Agency of Theory

Althusser reconstructs theory (or philosophy) as a *process of knowledge production without a subject*. The production of knowledge is framed as an intra-conceptual process governed by (à la Cavaillès) axiomatic rules internal to the process of conceptual production itself. Althusser spells this out in "On the Materialist Dialectic." There Althusser lays out a theory of "Three Generalities" to schematically theorize the process of scientific knowledge production.[33]

Generality I is the "raw material" of a given scientific theory. An example of this would be classical political economy. Generality II is a process of transforming this material by theoretical production. Principally this process concerns ridding Generality I of its ideological admixtures. This transformed material rid of ideological baggage produces Generality III. An example of this is Marx's *Capital*. Just as Marx began not with empirical glosses on capitalism, but with the findings of classical political economy (i.e., Generality I), so too Althusser and his students began with Marx's *Capital* (i.e., Generality III) in order to develop historical and dialectical materialism in a scientific direction.

The process of generality production would seem to necessitate confronting again the problem of the subject. Who or what works on the raw material of a generality? Althusser in the same essay writes:

> But *who* or *what* is it that works? What should we understand by the expression: the science works? As we have seen, every transformation of a raw material into products works by setting in motion determinate means of production. What is the moment, the level or the instance which corresponds to the means of production, in the theoretical practice of science? If we abstract from men in these means of production for the time being, it is what I shall call the *Generality II*, constituted by the corpus of concepts whose more or less contradictory unity constitutes the "theory" of the science at the (historical) moment under consideration, the "theory" that defines the field in which all the problems of the science must necessarily be posed ... We must rest content with these schematic gestures and not enter into the dialectic of this theoretical labor.[34]

Althusser sidesteps the thorny question of "the dialectic of this theoretical labor" productive of theoretical knowledge and chooses to "rest content" instead with "schematic gestures." Althusser "gestures" toward a "materialist dialectic" of knowledge as production, but he must "rest content" with schematism in place of a general materialist theory of theoretical labor because this would require accounting for the place of the knowledge laborer in the production of knowledge.[35] Althusser notes that the "work by which Generality I becomes Generality III ... only involves the process of theoretical practice, that is, it all takes place 'within knowledge.'"[36]

What does it mean to be entirely "within knowledge?" Does not this commit his theory to a strict separation of knowledge from the world and thereby consign his theory to idealism? Yes and no. Althusser holds to a Spinozist distinction between materiality and intelligibility understood as a distinction between differing modes of one fundamental "substance." The "substance" that secures the relation between the object of knowledge and the real object is historical-materialist science. But there is something more than Spinozist theory that drives Althusser's epistemology—politics.

Althusser's *theory of theory* is a political corrective to Marxism-humanism operative in Communist theory and politics post-1956. The resurrection of the human subject in Marxist-humanism is for Althusser a sign of liberal creep. Althusser notes this explicitly in "To My English Readers" in *For Marx*:

> The critique of Stalinist "dogmatism" was generally "lived" by Communist intellectuals as a "liberation." This "liberation" gave birth to a profound ideological reaction, "liberal" and "ethical" in tendency, which spontaneously rediscovered the old philosophical themes of "freedom," "man," the "human person," and "alienation." This ideological tendency looked for theoretical justification to Marx's Early Works, which do indeed contain all the arguments of

a philosophy of man, his alienation and liberation. ... Marx's Early Works have been a war-horse for petty bourgeois intellectuals in their struggle against Marxism; but little by little, and then massively, they have been set to work in the interests of a new "interpretation" of Marxism which is today being openly developed by many Communist intellectuals, "liberated" from Stalinist dogmatism by the Twentieth Congress.[37]

Panagiotis Sotiris argues that Althusser's theoretical anti-humanism is through and through a political project. His rejection of "humanism" is a counterstrike against party "liberalization" wrought by de-Stalinization. Post-Stalinist reformism licensed a return to the early Marx's writings. The early works on alienation, on freedom, and on man affirm the liberalism of Marxism's enemies. Althusser sees it as a political duty not to allow the Young Marx to set the theoretical orientation of contemporary Communism. The scientific Marx alone provides the means to construct a philosophy of Communist commitment.

Communist politics for Althusser is not a matter of personal opinion, taste, or any other liberal conception of commitment. It is first and foremost a commitment to the engine of working-class emancipation: the party. Politics without the party, for Althusser, is a nonstarter. "Since he thought there could be no politics outside the Communist Party and its relations with the working class," writes Sotiris, Althusser "opted for a strategy of theoretical correction of a strategic crisis, based on a theoretical and philosophical reconstruction of Marx's authority."[38] Put simply: Althusser sought to return the Communist Parties to their founding Marxist orientation. The PCF's embrace of Khrushchev's *Marxism with a human face* unleashed a liberal-ideological figure of "man," which risked licensing a retreat from *Marx* in the name of a de-Stalinized *Marxism*. Althusser in response instituted a kind of theoretical zero-tolerance policy on affirmative talk of the subject in order to check the spread of this liberal-reformist ideology in the name of a return to Marx's science.

A science of politics (Marxism) knows no subject. "There is no such thing as a *subject* of science," writes Althusser, "as far as scientific discourse, scientific statements, are concerned ... they can do without any kind of subject."[39]

Althusser *correct line* bars him according even a special status to Marx's (the man's) discoveries. It "is not Marx who says what the classical text [of classical political economy] does not," writes Althusser in *Reading Capital*, "it is the classical text itself which tells us that it is silent: its silence is *its own words*."[40] What then is it that makes Marx's revelation possible?

Althusser's answer: *theory*. "It is ... [not] the eye (the mind's eye) of a subject which *sees* what exists in the field defined by a theoretical problematic," writes Althusser, "it is this field itself which *sees itself* in the objects or problems it defines."[41] Here we see quite literally Cavaillès' *philosophy of the concept* in action. Philosophy operationalizes a theoretical "sighting" through the immanent definition of its objects and problems. For example, two plus two equals four as a function of the way that the numbers and the operational relation between them are axiomatically defined. Whatever a subject might think about this has no bearing on its truth content.

Althusser's science-ideology distinction during the mid-1960s rests, notes Peden, on "the relationship of concepts to their objects. Ideology receives its objects whereas science generates them."[42] Thus, for Althusser, Marx was right to study capitalism *not* by stepping out of the British Museum into the dank air of industrial London but instead by patiently studying the texts of classical political economy. Marx started with classical political economy because its half-baked science *is half-baked*. This gave him a starting point for the critical reconstruction of a scientifically more adequate account of capitalism. Likewise, Althusser (and his students) follow Marx's example by starting with *Capital* to construct the necessary scientific coordinates for an understanding of capitalism. "Althusser wants to understand how

Capital works," notes Peden, "and by extension understand something about how 'capital' works."[43] But, having noted this, Peden rightly asks:

> It is uncertain what is more striking about this theoretical conclusion, the dizzying level of philosophical thought needed to arrive at it or the simplicity of its implications. For what Althusser has shown ... is simply that what we experience as our lives is nothing more than an "effect" of something else that is not in reality a *something* else at all but the contingent, accumulation of all the preceding "effects" convergent in a temporal moment or spatial point.[44]

The empiricist (ideological) concept of knowledge rests on the idea that reality (of capitalism, our lives, etc.) need only be "recognized." Science by contrast is a process that *generates an object of knowledge* to account precisely for what is passively recognized as reality. *Subjects recognize reality; science produces knowledge of reality.*

The question of the subject had to be repressed in *For Marx* and *Reading Capital* in order to correct the reformist line of Marxism-humanism. The symptomatic silence on the subject in Althusser's theoreticist conception of theoretical production signaled the need for a theory of the subject, of its formation, and deformation, of its structuring by material and historical processes. This is the matter Althusser tentatively attempts to work out in the ISAs essay of 1970.

Notes

1. Quoted in Georges Labica, *Marxism and the Status of Philosophy*, trans. Kate Soper and Martin Ryle (Sussex: The Harvester Press, 1980), 288.
2. Ibid.
3. Karl Marx and Frederick Engels, *The German Ideology*, in *Collected Works, Vol. 5, 1845–1847* (New York: International Publishers, 2018), 36.
4. Sarah Kofman, *Camera Obscura: Of Ideology*, trans. Will Straw (Ithaca: Cornell University Press, 1999), 4.

5   Karl Marx, *Capital*, Vol. I, in *Collected Works*, Vol. 35 (New York: International Publishers, 2017), 83.
6   Nick Nesbitt, *The Price of Slavery: Capitalism and Revolution in the Caribbean* (Charlottesville, Virginia: University of Virginia Press, 2022), 77.
7   Alfred Sohn-Rethel, *Intellectual and Manual Labor*, trans. Martin Sohn-Rethel (Leiden: Brill, 2021), 39.
8   See Knox Peden, *Spinoza Contra Phenomenology: French Rationalism from Cavaillès to Deleuze* (Stanford: Stanford University Press, 2014).
9   Knox Peden, "'Autonomy, Therefore Necessity:' Jean Cavaillès's Contribution to a Theory of Science," in Jean Cavaillès, *On Logic and the Theory of Science*, trans. Robin Mackay and Knox Peden (New York: Urbanomic/Sequence Press, 2021), 3.
10 Ibid., 14.
11 Cavaillès, *On Logic and the Theory of Science*, 66.
12 Ibid.
13 Ibid.
14 Georges Canguilhem and Charles Ehresmann, "Editors' Notice," in Cavaillès, *On Logic and the Theory of Science*, 31–2.
15 Peden, *Spinoza Contra Phenomenology*, 19.
16 Ibid.
17 Ibid., 20.
18 Ibid.
19 See Peter Hallward and Knox Peden, eds. *Concept and Form, Volume 1: Key Texts from the* Cahiers pour l'Analyse (London: Verso, 2012); and Peter Hallward and Knox Peden, eds. *Concept and Form, Volume 2: Interviews and Essays on the* Cahiers pour l'Analyse (London: Verso, 2012).
20 Mao Tse-Tung, *On the Correct Handling of Contradictions among the People* (Peking: Foreign Language Press, 1966), 30. Note that I use the "Z" spelling for "Zedong" whereas Foreign Language Press publications use "Tse- Tung."
21 Louis Althusser, et al., *Reading Capital: The Complete Edition*, trans. Ben Brewster and David Fernbach (London: Verso, 2015), 52.
22 Peter Hallward, "Introduction: Theoretical Training," in Hallward and Peden, eds. *Concept and Form, Volume 1*, 22.

23 "A Philosophical Conjuncture: An Interview with Etienne Balibar and Yves Duroux," in Hallward and Peden, *Concept and Form, Volume 2*, 174.
24 Ibid.
25 Quoted in Knox Peden, "Introduction: The Fate of the Concept," in Hallward and Peden, eds. *Concept and Form, Volume 2*, 6.
26 Althusser, *Reading Capital*, 35.
27 Ibid., 39.
28 Ibid., 38.
29 Ibid., 35.
30 Ibid.
31 Quoted in Gregory Elliott, *Althusser: The Detour of Theory* (Chicago: Haymarket Books, 2009), 170.
32 Ibid.
33 See Louis Althusser, "On the Materialist Dialectic," in *For Marx*, trans. Ben Brewster (New York: Vintage Books, 1970).
34 Ibid., 184–5.
35 Alain Badiou has noted the "dangerous" idealism in Althusser's early theory of theoretical production. See Alain Badiou, "The Althusserian Definition of 'Theory,'" in *The Concept in Crisis: Reading Capital Today*, ed. Nick Nesbitt (Durham: Duke University Press, 2017).
36 Althusser, "On the Materialist Dialectic," 185.
37 Louis Althusser, "To My English Readers," in *For Marx*, 10–11.
38 Panagiotis Sotiris, *A Philosophy of Communism: Rethinking Althusser* (Chicago: Haymarket Books, 2021), 349.
39 Louis Althusser, "Three Notes on the Theory of Discourses," in *The Humanist Controversy and Other Writings*, ed. François Matheron and G. M. Goshgarian (London: Verso, 2003), 77.
40 Althusser, *Reading Capital*, 20.
41 Ibid., 24.
42 Peden, *Spinoza Contra Phenomenology*, 147.
43 Ibid., 157.
44 Ibid., 171.

3

Althusser (Part II)

Structure against Subject

Althusser's theoretical effort to construct an anti-humanist epistemology was also a political correction to what he deemed the ideological drift named "Marxism-humanism." This theoretical-political corrective consists of a strategic conflation of "human" and "subject." This conflation marks not only the 1965 texts, but his later work of self-criticism. For example, in "Reply to John Lewis," Althusser insists that Marxist theory is rooted in material conditions.

Althusser in fact draws close to economism in his articulation of the materialist basis of class struggle. The class struggle "does not go on in the air, or on something like a football pitch," writes Althusser; it "is rooted in the mode of production and exploitation in a given class society."[1] He continues:

> This materiality [of class struggle], in the last instance, is at the same time the "base" … of the class struggle, and its material existence; because exploitation takes place in production, and it is exploitation which is at the root of the antagonism between the classes and of the class struggle. It is this profound truth which Marxism-Leninism expresses in the well-known Thesis of class struggle in the infrastructure, in the "economy," in class exploitation—and in the Thesis that *all the forms of the class struggle are rooted in economic class struggle*. It is on this condition that the revolutionary thesis of the primacy of class struggle is a materialist one.[2]

Materialist science, according to Althusser, knows nothing of "man" or the "subject." It knows only the materialist basis of classed society and the struggle immanent to that social form. "Man" would only be an infrastructural (or superstructural) effect of this materialist base. Any inquiry that begins with *man* or the *human subject* starts from a nonmaterialist standpoint that by definition is unscientific and thus ideological. Althusser here sets the stage for the memorable passage—a passage that passes—from the materialist thesis of class struggle to the thesis that there is no "subject" from the standpoint of materialist history. A clear-eyed conception of materialist history should dispel the illusory question of the subject. Althusser writes:

> When that is clear [the materialist basis of history], the question of the "subject" of history disappears. History is an immense *natural-human* system in movement, and the motor of history is class struggle. History is a process, and a *process without a subject*. The question about how "*man makes history*" disappears altogether. Marxist theory rejects it once and for all; it sends it back to its birthplace: bourgeois ideology.[3]

History is an "immense *natural-human* system in movement," which is to say that it is a mobile nature-culture hybrid. But this system is subject to something else that is not properly a subject: movement, the motor of which is class struggle. Thus the "human" is invoked as a figure in the nature-culture couplet, but not as the motor force of this system in movement. For Althusser, Marxist science is the mechanics (or movement) of the material base of society whose movement articulates and transforms the definition of that subject called the "human."

Structure to Subject

The question of the subject became a pivot point around which revolved both Althusser's devoted students and his most vocal critics. Was an Althusserian theory of agency and militant commitment possible? Did anti-humanism render that question meaningless? His critics answered in the affirmative. The historian E. P. Thompson, for one, accused Althusser of having obscured the role of revolutionary subjectivity and impassioned commitment by a haze of theory produced by intellectuals safely ensconced in the École Normale Supérieure.[4] The French Communist Party (PCF) also took aim. Their leading polemicist of the day (and later Holocaust denier), Roger Garaudy, accused Althusser of failing to acknowledge the "active element." He writes:

> Althusser's "theoretical anti-humanism" … rests on the illusion of being able to entrench oneself in the concept and so treat structures and social relationships without reference to human options. This eliminates the "active element" of knowledge so forcibly emphasized by Marx as being the "subjective" (but in no way individualist) element of historical initiative—the active element of consciousness which is inherent in the very principle of a revolutionary party.[5]

Reading this passage one can more readily grasp Althusser's frustration with the PCF's intellectuals. The confused mélange of concepts— "human options," "active element," "historical initiative," "the active element of consciousness" (is there any form of consciousness that is not "active")—is symptomatic of a profound theoretical disorientation. The assumption that the mission of a revolutionary party is to catalyze "the active element of consciousness" or the "subjective" dimension of commitment surely makes sense at a certain level. The party should inspire. But it should also *think*. And what it could not think it seems is that the very concept of "consciousness" and the "subjective element" are precisely historical structures whose debt to bourgeois-liberal ideology has to be confronted rather than reverently repeated under the red banner.

Garaudy's cautionary parenthetical qualifier that the active element of consciousness is "in no way individualist" fails to explain how and why. Althusser's theory of theoretical practice at least has the virtue of attempting a coherent theory of politically committed knowledge production in theoretically anti-humanist terms. What Althusser's critics also forgot then (and some now) is that anti-humanism is always for Althusser "theoretical anti-humanism." The concept of the human—"human options" as it were—is not abandoned by Althusser tout court. The opening lines of *Reading Capital* fully acknowledge the "historical initiative" of class struggle. Althusser is not opposed to "human options," *but he is opposed to the options for theorizing what those options are according to the coordinates of liberal-bourgeois thought.*

It is also clear now in a way that was not as clear to outsiders then that many of Althusser's students sensed that the question of the subject—that "active element"—required theorization. The students who were involved with *Cahiers pour l'Analyse* were convinced that the theory of the subject had to be *reworked*. Jacques-Alain Miller, for example, notes in "Action of the Structure," published in 1968, that the theory of the subject should be derived from knowledge of the action of a structure (or structuring processes) without appeal to a fetishized notion of a special domain of the subject—in the realm of the "lived," "experience," and so on—or any such place beyond the "action" of structuring processes. "As understood here," writes Miller, "structure will not reserve a place for anything that might be above and beyond scientific discourse."[6] Models that place a distance between what can be scientifically known about the subject and "the subjective element" should "now disappear," writes Miller, "and an exact integration of the lived into the structural must now be made to operate."[7] Defining structure axiomatically, Miller writes: "Structure, then: that which puts in place an experience for the subject that it includes."[8]

Miller's approach works by "starting from structure" so as "to enter into the theory of the subject."[9] Miller suggests that it is theoretically possible and necessary to access an analytic point anterior to structured structures to grasp their historical structuration. From this anterior vantage, the subject appears as structured result of a process that can be theorized. "If therefore, against the philosophy of structuralism," writes Miller, "we require a notion of subjectivity, this subjectivity will figure not as regent but as subjected."[10] Here "subjected" does not precisely mean dominated. It means that subjectivity is not a free exercise of boundless "human options," but rather that those "options" are structured by something anterior to subjective experience. The "task of the theory of the subject," notes Miller, is "first of all to refute the phenomenological attempt to rediscover the naïve or primitive state" of consciousness, experience, or lived life.[11] What is needed is an "archaeological" account of precisely how "subjectivity" and its liberal theses were constituted and achieved the appearance of a foundation. "The work of Michel Foucault," Miller concludes, "today gives us the first example of such an archaeology."[12]

Miller's novel reorientation of structuralism—a *structuralism of the subject*—took the Foucauldian path not to the historical archives but toward a theory of the subject heterogeneous to that structured result identified as the "individual" in liberal-bourgeois thought. The theory of the subject would require first a dismantling of the "individual." But the second move would require producing an adequate concept of the revolutionary subject. This reconstructed concept of subject would be composed of a diverse set of raw conceptual materials: the Leninist concept of the full-time revolutionary, the Maoist concept of the cadre, and a militantly Cavaillèsian commitment to science. Miller affirms Bachelard's call to *work the concept* and Althusser's stipulation that conceptualization is a form of production. Althusser writes:

> The whole of this conceptual labor will adopt as its slogan Georges Canguilhem's definition: "To work a concept is to vary its extension and comprehension, to generalize it through the incorporation of

exceptional traits, to export it beyond its region of origin, to take it as a model or on the contrary to seek a model for it—to work a concept, in short, is progressively, to confer upon it, through regulated transformations, the function of a form."[13]

Condensed in this "slogan" is a uniquely political conception of epistemology. First, Miller takes Bachelard's statement as a "slogan." Bachelard's definition of a concept is reworked and its extension varied. The statement no longer belongs to the discipline of epistemology alone. It belongs to a task of "conceptual labor" at once philosophical and political. For here it is precisely a matter of working the concept of the subject to vary it and "extend it beyond its region of origin" in the matrix of liberal thought. The models here are psychoanalysis and Marxism.

The discipline of psychoanalysis extended and transformed the meaning of ordinary words such as "sexuality," "real," "other," and so on into an analytic theory. Likewise, Marxism extended and transformed vague notions taken from classical political economy such as "commodity," "labor," "value," "exchange," and so on. Miller suggests that a truly rigorous concept attains the status of "form"—like Marx's concept of "money-form"—by achieving an equilibrium between generality of meaning and specificity of use. A conceptual form should be able to capture a range of phenomena equally well, but in a regulated way that is governed by the immanent rules of applicability established by the very coherence of the theory. To construct a rigorous concept therefore requires the construction of a theory that regulates the meaning and use of that concept. To construct a concept of the subject *ergo sum* requires a theory of the subject.

Miller shows that there is no inherent contradiction between structure and subject. These are terms that must be reworked into concepts that as such will extend their remit beyond the domains of existing structuralism and the liberal formulations of the subject. Miller's break with structuralism is not simply "poststructuralism" as it has come down to us. His task is different. This task does not shy from the demand to produce a coherent even systematic theory. It takes that demand as a political duty. This conviction was forged in the crucible of Maoist theory and practice then on the march.

Althusser's Cultural Revolution

In 1966, Althusser anonymously published a short text on the Cultural Revolution. Althusser there approves of the Cultural Revolution *in practice*. He sees it as a practical repudiation of economistic or vulgar Marxism. But he holds that the correct way to respond to the Cultural Revolution is to translate the fact of its existence into a *properly Marxist theory*. Althusser writes that the Cultural Revolution "is not, first of all, an argument: it is first and foremost an *historical fact*."[14] The fact of the Cultural Revolution, as an "unprecedented fact" requires theorization in order to render this historical fact part of the theoretical science of historical materialism. For, as Althusser warns us:

> [I]t is impermissible to […] take a position [on the Cultural Revolution] without a serious examination beforehand. A communist cannot, from the distance where we stand, make pronouncements about the C.R. [Cultural Revolution], and therefore *judge* it, without having analyzed, at least in principle, the political and theoretical credentials of the C.R. … in light of Marxist principles.[15]

In other words, what is needed is not simply a political affirmation of the Cultural Revolution but a Marxist-Leninist (not Maoist) theorization that would make possible a philosophical and political judgment of it. Althusser writes, "[W]e must examine this political fact [of the Cultural Revolution] in light of Marxist theoretical principles (historical materialism, dialectical materialism), asking ourselves whether this political fact is, or is not, in conformity with these theoretical principles."[16] Althusser denies any theoretical novelty to the Maoist idea of Cultural Revolution. Althusser notes that it was Lenin who first "spoke openly of the vital necessity of cultural revolution."[17] Thus the Maoist revolution in culture is theoretically translated into the "orthodoxy" of Marxism-Leninism.

Althusser returned to the Cultural Revolution in lectures later published as *Philosophy and the Spontaneous Philosophy of the Scientists*. There he strikes an ambivalent tone. On the one hand, he effusively praises the "grandeur of Mao" and he applauds his theory of contradiction as applied to the contradiction between party and masses.[18] But, still, he does not accord Maoism any real *theoretical* significance. Althusser writes:

> This is what constitutes the grandeur of Mao: that he practically questioned the metaphysical idea of the dialectic by audaciously submitting the dialectic to the dialectic (in his theory of "contradiction"), and he thus broached the nature of ideological relations and put his finger on the separation and power of the party apparatus, in the ambitious project of a cultural revolution, designed to change the relation between Party and the masses. Here too, however, practice did not lead to a theory.[19]

Maoism pushed the dialectic one step beyond by electrifying the political-power antagonism between masses and party. Maoism in practice redefined class struggle within socialism as a more purely ideological struggle between the ageing "Party bourgeoisie" and militant youth. The conflict was not over economic "base" but cultural "superstructure." The Cultural Revolution put the lie to economism. A socialist economy does not itself secure socialist society. "Base" does not determine "superstructure" and hence the need for Cultural Revolution. Althusser notes that the Cultural Revolution was "designed to change the relation between Party and the masses," but "this practice did not lead to theory." Althusser affirms a strict division between theory and practice. Despite its Marxist "credentials," this division is nothing more than a Leftist version of capital's division between intellectual and manual labor. Althusser's text slyly moves from a patronizing gesture of praise for the practice of the Cultural Revolution to a call to construct a general theory of "cultural revolution." Althusser here settles his accounts with the Chinese in his affirmation of Marxist-Leninist theory over Maoist practice. For indeed, it is Mao who holds that practice is the primary source of political ideas. No doubt Althusser cannot take seriously Mao's essay "On Practice" of 1937.

Mao holds that Marxism-Leninism *is an empirical science*. "The dialectical-materialist theory of knowledge places practice in the primary position," writes Mao, "holding that human knowledge can in no way be separated from practice and repudiating all the erroneous theories which deny the importance of practice or separate knowledge from practice."[20] Mao invokes Lenin to authorize his empirical theory of knowledge. "Thus Lenin said: 'Practice is higher than (theoretical) knowledge, for it has not only the dignity of universality, but also of immediate actuality.'"[21] Practice is higher because it takes place in actuality. Theory is a second-order practice. "The Marxist philosophy of dialectical materialism has two outstanding characteristics," writes Mao; one "is its class nature: it openly avows that dialectical materialism is in the service of the proletariat. The other is its practicality: it emphasizes the dependence of theory on practice, emphasizes that theory is based on practice and in turn serves practice."[22] Marxist philosophy is a philosophy of practice. We must not forget that Althusser did break with "theoreticism" in *Essays in Self-Criticism*. Thereafter he affirms that theory is fundamentally determined by the practice of class struggle. His master formula (really slogan) becomes: "philosophy represents the people's class in theory."[23] But even here one can detect that Althusser gives theory the upper hand. It is theory that "represents" the class struggle. Theory not struggle itself systematizes and determines the meaning of that which is determinant of historical change: class struggle.

Subject of Maoism

French Maoism of the 1960s continues to attract historical and theoretical interest. Richard Wolin, for one, is quite critical of the phenomenon. He sees it as principally a history of political exoticization of Mao by Western political activists and artists.[24] The latter is a crucial point in his argument. Wolin claims that French radicals reduced an actual revolution in China to a set of signs and slogans that advertised radicality without the attendant risks. Wolin argues that French Maoism was principally a matter of aesthetics rather than politics. He holds up Badiou as an especially egregious example. Wolin claims that the thought of Badiou (and others) amounts to a kind of aestheticization of politics. Taking Walter Benjamin's well-known formula—*aestheticization of politics equals fascism*—Wolin holds that Badiou's supposed reduction of Maoism to an aesthetics of thought is a cover for authoritarianism and is thus a moral failure not unlike Heidegger's embrace of Nazism about which Wolin has also written extensively.[25] Both cases represent for Wolin a dangerous and irresponsible fascination with authoritarianism that cannot and should not be separated from the philosophy of such thinkers. Wolin's further political argument is that the French Left destroyed its relevancy by touting an impossibly idealized and exoticized ideology, the reality of which it willfully refused to understand. French Maoists, he argues, wrongly embraced an ideology that was impossible to institute and thus it spared the young radicals the risk of failure or worse.

Wolin historicizes Maoism in China, for its part, as case of the violent propagandization of the population for the sake of stabilizing and extending Mao's grip on the Chinese Communist Party (CCP). The French variant, on Wolin's reading, simply copied Mao's images and slogans; a hollow, simulacral double of the politics of the former. Wolin misses the crucial role that signs, images, and even fashion played in the political articulation of both French and Chinese Maoism. Wolin's Benjaminian concern with the fascist aestheticization of politics forgets that Benjamin also advocated for communist *politicization of art*.[26] Much ink has been spilled on trying to parse the difference between these positions, but we might simply say as a start that *communism*—and here Benjamin follows Marx and Engels— is a movement not a final state of affairs that abolishes the existing (capitalist) order. Politicizing art (and aesthetics) would be a process of emancipating aesthetics from its enclosed position within the liberal ideology of *art for art's sake*. No longer would aesthetics be a means of preserving aesthetic tradition or traditional (and reactionary) forms of power such as fascism but instead would be a means of transforming both life and art by a real emancipatory movement.

Wolin problematically conflates Mao with Mao*ism*. Whatever Mao's intentions in unleashing the Cultural Revolution, the revolution exceeded his control. Consider the case of the Red Guards. Formed in 1966, it was first composed of elite cadres who came from families with impeccable party credentials. But this elitist organization was opposed by rebel groups who set about to destroy the party elite and *its* mass organizations. Rebel groups saw themselves as true to the spirit of Maoist thought in their militant opposition to the party bourgeoisie who enjoyed wealth and privileges denied the masses. The Red Guard rebel groups were not blindly loyal.

This popular (and liberal) view simply repeats the stereotype of the passive Asian subject. It fails to recognize the *creative initiative* that is in fact the hallmark of Maoist thought and action.

Laikwan Pang has shown in her brilliant study, *The Art of Cloning: Creative Production during China's Cultural Revolution*, that the stereotyped image of "brainwashed" masses seduced by Mao's "cult of personality" is a Western myth marked by the limits of bourgeois individualism and poisoned by orientalist racism.[27] Pang (like Althusser) finds the "cult of personality" a pseudo-concept. It fails to capture the subtle dialectic between the immanence of revolution and its incarnation in the image of the transcendent leader. It also fails to register the *aesthetic revolution accomplished by the Cultural Revolution.*

Mao was largely an abstraction for most revolutionaries. He was more a signifier than a person. He was a distant figure whose portrait they hung on their walls and whose slogans they committed to memory. It is precisely this gap between the masses and Mao that afforded the space for the exercise of revolutionary creativity. Mao's figure was a floating signifier, the meaning of which was adapted to the needs of the struggle that the young rebels waged against the party bureaucracy and the cultural foundations of "old" China.

Furthermore, we should bear in mind that as early as 1967, Mao admitted that he was no longer in control of the direction of the Cultural Revolution or of the meaning of his images. Pang shows, for example, that Mao tried to stop the building of Mao statues except those approved by the central arm of the Cultural Revolution Group. But this effort entirely failed. Instead, groups competed with one another to build taller and taller statues. The publication and dissemination of *The Little Red Book* is also a case study in mass initiative. The book edited by Lin Biao and bound in red vinyl like an army field manual is a select set of quotations from Mao's speeches and writings. The book, however, came in time to function as a largely autonomous text replete with its own meanings.[28] Even to be seen holding the physical book itself eventually functioned as a political sign. To cite another instance where Maoist initiative outflanked Mao's control, Pang notes in November 1967 that "a central government circular was issued stating that no one could reprint any unpublished photo of the Chairman."²⁹ But this effort radically failed. Two years later, the central authority "explicitly forbade formalistic worship of the Chairman as well as the unauthorized printing of his image or works," but this failed too.³⁰ The words and image of Mao were no longer his own. His authority and authorial function were swept away by the course of the revolution. "Mao" was a floating signifier for immanent cultural struggle and not a master signifier of preestablished truths. "People worshiped Mao," notes Pang, "but they were also aware that it was the people around them who gave Mao these meanings."³¹ This is "worship" then of a sort that the pseudo-concept of "cult of personality" obscures. This "worship" operated in two directions according to Pang: "vertical worship facilitated horizontal comradeship."³² "The notion of the Mao cult," notes Pang, "does not have the analytic power to explore what the sudden popularity of ... [Mao] propaganda meant in the initiation of the revolution."³³ The notion of the "cult of personality" attributes magical powers to images and it attributes child-like naiveté to those who revered them. Moreover, this pseudo-concept obscurely Christianizes and demeans revolutionaries who placed their faith not in transcendence but in concrete struggle. The image of the leader, the slogan, the party badge defies the bland Western ideology of hyper-individualism, which is incapable of conceptualizing the revolutionary dialectic between individual initiative and collective struggle, between personal commitment and transpersonal solidarity, between individual thought and party line, between spontaneous rebellion and disciplined action.

The concept of the "cult of personality" is not a properly theoretical concept. It substitutes the extraordinarily complicated historical sequences of the CPSU between 1924 and 1953 and of China between 1967 and 1976 with a nonhistorical construct drawn from the rhetoric of humanism and religious zeal. Khrushchev invoked the "cult of personality" to explain Stalin's terror. But he explained nothing. He merely applied an ill-fitting label to the Stalinist period. Althusser writes:

> Now this pseudo-concept ["the cult of personality"], the circumstances of whose solemn and dramatic pronouncement [at the Twentieth Congress of the CPSU] are well known did indeed expose certain practices: "abuses," "errors," and in certain cases "crimes." But it explained nothing of their conditions, of their causes, in short of their *internal* determination, and therefore of their forms. Yet since it *claimed* to explain what it in fact it did not explain, this pseudo-concept could only mislead those whom it was supposed to instruct.[34]

The "cult of personality" is a perfectly humanist notion. And that's why it fails. Humanism is wedded to the conceptual constellation of individualism: persons, personhood, personality, persona, and so on. As such it is blind to anything like socialism that by definition cannot be accounted for by the conceptual resources of individualism. Not only does this pseudo-concept—"cult of personality"—fail to explain. It also exonerates. Its effects are therefore twofold: ideological (humanism) and juridical (exoneration). To reduce the Maoist period or the Stalinist period to the personality cult of a single man entirely exonerates the party, civil society, and as well as Stalinist and Maoist theory. The pseudo-concept also provided the perfect ideological weapon for Western liberals eager to denounce the Chinese Cultural Revolution. Their denunciation of Mao's "cult of personality" reduced the militancy of thousands of committed revolutionaries to unthinking subjects. It projected a purely orientalist image of their innocence that is as offensive as it is false. The thesis of the "cult of personality" applied to the Cultural Revolution is also quite ironic in that the revolution was precisely a revolution against bourgeois culture's fascination with "personality" as well as the religiosity of "old" China. And let's not forget that the party was the central target of the Cultural Revolution. The young militants refused to allow the

1949 Revolution to be eclipsed by the Party bourgeoisie of the 1960s. To "explain" this complicated process as simply a case of the "cult of personality" does violence to the history of the Cultural Revolution. And let us remember that the Cultural Revolution is not only a history of violence. It is also the history of all that was hoped and struggled for by those militant rebels who refused to take the "capitalist road." I am not exonerating those who committed reprehensible acts of violence. Precisely, I am holding them responsible as I am the many others who earnestly pursued the task of Cultural Revolution. We should hold both parties accountable *as revolutionaries* and not as unthinking masses seduced by the cult of Mao as orientalist ideology has it. We must understand the complexity of the "Mao" signifier.

The name "Mao," notes Badiou, is "intrinsically contradictory in the field of revolutionary politics."[35] It is "contradictory" because "Mao" names at once the man who for a time was the supreme leader of the most powerful Communist Party next to that of the Soviet Union. But at the same time, "Mao" names the revolt against that Party. Badiou continues:

> "Mao" is the name of a paradox: the rebel in power, the dialectician put to the test by the continuing needs of "development," the emblem of the party-state in search of its overcoming, the military chief preaching disobedience to the authorities … This is what has given his "cult" a frenetic appearance, because subjectively he accumulated the accord given to the stately pomp of the Stalinist type, together with the enthusiasm of the entire revolutionary youth for the old rebel who cannot be satisfied with the existing state of affairs, and who wants to move on in the march to real communism. "Mao" was the name for the "construction of socialism," but also for its destruction.[36]

"Mao" names the institution of a dialectical contradiction between state and revolution. And it is the name for a revolution in militant style. I do not mean to be facetious here. The style of Maoism—the

"Mao suites," the portraits, the slogans—all this aesthetic paraphernalia should not be dismissed as *mere* fashion. It was integral to the constitution of a new form of subjectivity: the Maoist militant. The claim that the masses of young rebels and educated youth in China and France were simply posing is to deny the reality of their revolutionary agency. Their mode of public presentation was a medium through which they forged a new image of revolution. Their very look revolutionized the culture of revolutionary action itself. This aesthetic revolution was a politically necessary task in the eyes of the cultural revolutionaries and it is one of their lasting international legacies. Pang writes:

> The Cultural Revolution was a time when new looks were both suppressed and encouraged. Fashion in general was prohibited, and the people knew very well how politically risky it could be if they appeared different. But the revolution was also all about a new look, and the reordering of appearance was the most powerful way to express a reordering of the ideological and material world.[37]

We need to bear this in mind when considering the case of French Maoism in the 1960s. It is all too easy to dismiss the youth in the streets with their Mao portraits, badges, or *Little Red Books* as simply a case of revolutionary chic. That dismissal misses a crucial fact. First, there was (is) a Maoist aesthetic. Second, this aesthetic was part and parcel of the politics of the Cultural Revolution. The young students around Althusser like Badiou, Rancière, and Miller were looking east lured by this novel aesthetic-political-theoretical formation: Maoism. No doubt their view was tinged with orientalism. But it was also informed by a longing for internationalism and a conviction that "Mao" named a revolution in Communist theory that could be used to go beyond the sclerotic politics of the French Communist Party. Above all, Maoism offered young French radicals a new theory of the subject. Maoism celebrates the subjective factor (á la Garaudy), but it also celebrates the disciplined destruction of the subjective factor as articulated by bourgeois philosophy. It reimagined subjective experience by suturing it to a revolution in the very meaning of "subjective experience" as canonized by bourgeois aesthetics and politics. "Maoism" names the reorganization of the subjective-objective couplet into a new theoretical matrix in which collectivity and individuality are no longer opposed as they are in bourgeois ideology. Maoism names the possibility of the "I" of subjective initiative constructed and claimed in its suture to collective becoming. To be a Maoist is to be one of many. But it is also to be one.

It is therefore unsurprising that Badiou would in 1980 publish *Theory of the Subject*. Comprised of material delivered as lectures in the 1970s, Badiou constructs a Maoist-Lacanian theory of the subject that takes the bourgeoisie-proletariat couplet as not only a structural dialectic but a *historical dialectic of force*. A theory of Communism must include a theory of force, argues Badiou, and not be content with the schematism of class and productive forces. Badiou writes:

> The famous contradiction of bourgeoisie/proletariat is a limited, structural scheme that loses track of the torsion of the Whole of which the proletariat *qua* subject traces the force. To say proletariat and bourgeoisie is to remain within the bounds of the Hegelian artifice: something and something else. Why? Because the project of the proletariat, its internal being, is not to contradict the bourgeoisie, or to cut its feet from under it. This project is communism and nothing else. That is the abolition of any place in which something like a proletariat can be installed. The political project of the proletariat is the disappearance of the space of the placement of classes.[38]

Theory of the Subject is Badiou's most Maoist book. And one sees it in full in this passage. The bourgeois-proletariat couplet is merely an idealist-structuralist (Hegelian) contradiction. The real motor of history is not logic but "force." Class struggle is not a matter of "resolving" the logical contradiction between bourgeoisie and proletariat. It is a matter of radically defeating the bourgeoisie and by that disappearing the logical contradiction between class positions, which is nothing more than the very form of bourgeois rule. The whole question for Badiou in this book is how to become forceful subjects or "militants" capable of motoring history. Whatever blocks militant subjectivation is part of what must be struggled against. Becoming militant is not a matter of becoming another self but of dissolving the bourgeois parameters of selfhood in the collective subject of militancy and revolutionary action. The generative force constitutive of militant solidarity is militant ideology. The challenge is not to dispel ideology in general but to radically defeat *bourgeois ideology*. Here he affirms Mao who identified the need for the ideological remolding of the intellectual class. Mao writes in 1957:

> It seems as if Marxism was once all the rage but is currently not so much in fashion. To counter these tendencies, we must strengthen our ideological and political work. Both students and intellectuals should study hard ... [and] they must make progress both ideologically and politically, which means that they should study Marxism-Leninism, current events and politics. Not to have a correct political point of view is like having no soul.[39]

The passing of the "fashion" of Marxism-Leninism is no doubt an oblique reference to the revisionism instituted by the Twentieth Congress of the CPSU. Mao sees study as a political-ideological necessity to equip oneself with the "correct political point of view." Most striking is his claim that to not have the correct political view is like "having no soul." Correct ideological molding equips one with a soul—a core conviction and form of subjectivity—that makes possible the subjectivation required of militants. Ideology "fashions" subjects. That is its political power.

We have made this detour through the Maoist concept of the subject in order to set the stage for Althusser's theory of interpellation. Althusser's *general theory of ideology*—a theory that claims to offer a universal and "eternal" definition of ideology—was not itself fashioned in eternity, but cut its teeth in the Maoist moment. Althusser (as usual) will invoke Marxism-Leninism in defense of his theory. But the Maoists invoked the same signifier in defense of a counter-model of ideology. Not false science, ideology for the Maoists is a battlefront in the "cause of the people" to invoke the name of the well-known Maoist newspaper in France at the time.

Althusser's ISAs essay frames ideology as subjection. The essay, however, offers no clear antidote. Having given up his earlier theoreticist project, he no longer appeals to the power of an independent "science" to dispel ideological mystification and clear the way for revolution. The ISAs essay is part of Althusser's politicist project in which the primacy of class struggle is claimed and theory is understood to be an ally in that partisan struggle. No longer is theory the neutral arbiter of the distinction between science and ideology. It is a weapon of class struggle. Yet this politicist program is symptomatically absent from the ISAs essay. In his attempt to construct a theory of "ideology in general," Althusser appears to revert to a theoreticist orientation in which ideology is an object of knowledge for theory or science. Never is there a hint that ideology might itself be a weapon of the proletariat and not simply a weapon in the service of its enemies. It is as if the Maoist moment has been historically and theoretically suppressed in the name of theoretical science. No thought is paid to the idea that just as ideology "recruits" subjects (by means of subjection) to the ideology of the capitalist state, so too might it be (as for the Maoists) a means to "recruit" cadres in the struggle for emancipation. Althusser figures subjectivation as simply domination and never (as with the Maoists) an instance of becoming revolutionary. The essay thereby affirms once again the science/ideology opposition of theoreticism.

A General Theory

Published in *Pensée*, Althusser's 1970 notes toward a "general theory" of ideology were composed of a montage of extracts from a larger text, *On the Superstructure (Law-State-Ideology)*, which was eventually abandoned. "Ideology and Ideological State Apparatuses: Notes Toward an Investigation" is a sketch for a possible outline for a "general theory" of ideology and the state. The production of subjects and the power of the state are reciprocally related. The state produces subjects and the subjugation of individuals reproduces state power.

Althusser begins with the question: what is it that reproduces labor power? He makes short work of the economistic answer: subsistence wages furnish the necessities for the life of the laborer. This explains only how a body continues to live so as to work. "I shall say that the reproduction of labor power requires not only a reproduction of skills," notes Althusser, "but also, at the same time, a reproduction of submission to the rules of the established order."[40] Here is the first indication of what ideology means in the essay. Ideology means "submission to the established order." The "established order" under capital means a classed society, the order of which is enforced by the capitalist state. This social-state arrangement is reproduced each time a worker returns to work and submits to the rule of exploitation. Each time the worker returns to work she reproduces the ideology of subjection. Working under capital signifies "mastery" of the "practice" of capitalist ideology. This is key. This is not a matter of consciousness. Ideology is materially fashioned in embodied acts of subjection to the ruling ideology of the capitalist state.

Althusser acknowledges that his theory must confront the entire base-superstructure metaphor of classical Marxism. Ideology according to that model is a superstructural phenomenon determined by the economic base. But Althusser argues that base economic production has to be reliably reproduced. And wages alone cannot reliably guarantee it.

Something more compelling is needed to reliably ensure the reproduction of labor power. The problem with the base-superstructure "metaphor" is that it is static. It does not capture the iterative reproduction of the conditions for production. Althusser therefore adopts another metaphor: the machine. "The State is a 'machine' of repression which enables the ruling classes ... to ensure their domination over the working class," writes Althusser, "thus enabling the former to subject the latter to the process of surplus-value extortion (i.e. capitalist exploitation)."[41] Althusser then broadens the metaphor to "what the Marxist classics have called *the State apparatus*."[42] This term "defines the State as a force of repressive execution and intervention," writes Althusser, "in the class struggle conducted by the bourgeoisie and its allies against the proletariat."[43] Through the mechanism of exploitation the capitalist state apparatus produces the ideology needed to reliably ensure the reproduction of the conditions for the production of capital.

Althusser notes that the metaphor of the machine or the "apparatus" is nonetheless limited by virtue of it *being a metaphor*. It is not a scientific concept. This "presentation" of the state as "apparatus" is "still partly descriptive." This is a watchword in the essay. The point of a theory—and these are but notes toward it—is to replace a descriptive presentation with a scientific one. Althusser writes:

> Whenever, in speaking of the metaphor of the edifice [base-superstructure] or of the Marxist theory of the State, I have said that these are descriptive conceptions or representations of their objects, I had no other ulterior critical motives. On the contrary, I have every grounds to think that great scientific discoveries cannot help but pass through the phase of what I shall call "*descriptive theory*."[44]

Descriptive theory is "necessary to the development" of scientific theory.[45] We might liken this to the relation of Michael Faraday to that of James Clerk Maxwell. Faraday described electromagnetism as a "field."

Maxwell mathematized this insight. Althusser in this sense positions himself as the inheritor of Marx's great insight. His task is to complete the scientific theory of state-ideology apparatuses for which Marx gave the descriptive formulation. To have described the state as a machine driven by the economy in the last instance "is, without a shadow of a doubt, the irreversible beginning of the theory."[46] Althusser sees his project as adding something to the existing Marxist theory of the state articulated most forcefully by Marx and Lenin. Althusser writes:

> To summarize the "Marxist theory of the State" on this point, it can be said that the Marxist classics have always claimed that (1) the State is the repressive State apparatus, (2) State power and State apparatus must be distinguished, (3) the objective of the class struggle concerns State power, and in consequence the use of the State apparatus by the classes (or alliance of classes or of fractions of classes) holding State power as a function of their class objectives, and (4) the proletariat must seize State power in order to destroy the existing bourgeois State apparatus and, in a first phase, replace it with a quite different proletarian, State apparatus, then in later phases set in motion a radical process, that of the destruction of the State (the end of State power, the end of every State apparatus).[47]

These four axioms of the Marxist theory of the state define the terrain of Althusser's problematic. The bourgeois state is the form of social order established and enforced by capital interests. State power is simply an expression of class power. But state power is theoretically distinguishable from the state apparatus. The state may have every repressive apparatus—military, police, courts, and so on—at its disposal but have only weak state power if, for example, those apparatuses are undersupplied or otherwise unreliable. The state is the locus of power—weak or strong—and it is therefore the chief objective of class struggle to seize it. To be a class in power in the first instance is to be a class in command of the state. Althusser here follows Lenin to the letter: the first objective of struggle is the seizure of the state. The proletarian seizure of the state is revolutionary to the extent that this act of seizure also destroys the functions of the bourgeois state machine—creation and defense of private property, the maintenance of labor exploitation, the valorization of value—which is to say the reproduction of the conditions for capitalist production. What Althusser will add to this classical description is a theory (or notes toward one) of what reproduces the working class's subjection to the capitalist state.

Althusser takes the base-superstructure metaphor as a descriptive theory of the state—the state as economically determined in the last instance—and replaces it with the machinic metaphor of the "apparatus." This revised description resets the trajectory for advance toward a "theory of ideology in general" or a *general theory*.[48] The classical Marxist theory of the state accounts for its repressive functions and how those functions reinforce and defend the class in power. But so as "to advance the theory of the State it is indispensable to take into account," notes Althusser, "another reality, which is clearly on the side of the (repressive) State apparatus, but must not be confused with it. I shall call this reality by its concept: *the ideological State apparatuses*."[49] Key here is that the "Ideological State Apparatuses" (ISAs) are "on the side of" the repressive State apparatus (RSA), but the two should not be confused. The State is repressive. That's its singular function. But that function is carried out in two different ways.

The RSA (in the singular) works by the application of direct violence. ISAs (in the plural) work by a set of institutions. The State exercises violence in the public domain through the imposition of military rule, the application of the law, and the regulation of public affairs. Althusser explicitly contrasts the public nature of the RSA with the private nature of the ISAs. It might therefore be surprising to find a good number of public institutions in his list of ISAs. He lists the following as examples of ISAs: churches, family, legal codes, political parties (and systems of power transfer such as elections), trade unions, communications industries, and cultural institutions. But Althusser's point is that ISAs work on the *private life* of individuals. ISAs shape one's self-understanding and that directly shapes the actions and behaviors one exhibits. Those actions and behaviors will either conform or not to the ideologies of the ISAs. To conform is to be recognized as a good ideological subject. To not conform is to be recognized as deviant, an outsider, a scandal, or even a revolutionary.

The ideological content relayed by the ISAs is not what interests Althusser. Each ISA relays specific ideologies. For example, today school relays the ideology that STEM fields (science, technology, math, and engineering) are more important than the "humanities." Christian churches teach that Jesus is the Christ. The Republican Party teaches that the 2020 US election was rigged. But such discrete ideologies are not Althusser's target. His aim is to establish provisionary reference points for a "theory of ideology in general." What the ISAs share in common—ideology in general—is a singular function: they produce subjects by subjecting individuals to their repressive force. Individuals become, to keep with our examples, Republicans, Christians, or STEM students. And one is judged to be a good or bad subject in the terms established and repressively reinforced by these institutions. One either passes or fails in STEM. One is either going to heaven or hell. One is either a real Republican or a RINO (Republican in Name Only).

However, despite there being a plurality of ISAs there is, for Althusser, one invariant element: the ruling ideology is the ideology of the ruling class. Althusser writes, "[D]espite its diversity," ideology is always "the ideology of 'the ruling class.'"[50] This idea Althusser takes from *The German Ideology*. "The ideas of the ruling class are in every epoch the ruling ideas," write Marx and Engels, "the ruling *material* force of society is at the same time its ruling *intellectual* force."[51] Capitalist society needs State power to stabilize its economic base as is especially evident in times of financial crisis. Why does the State step in at such times to save the system? Because the State and capital are inextricably linked. The fate of one is the fate of the other. Neither Marx nor Althusser imagines that the bourgeoisie are master manipulators of ideological production. The bourgeoisie reproduces their ideological rule by what appears to them as commonsense and not as a set of class-specific ideas. The bourgeoisie sees individualism, possessiveness, acquisitiveness, and so on as universal human values. Hence, even the ruling class is ruled by ideology inasmuch as it does not recognize the class-specific character of its intellectual production. Ideological production has then a curious feature. The production of ideology never appears as ideology to the subjects it subjugates. "That is why those who are in ideology," writes Althusser, "believe themselves by definition outside ideology: one of the effects of ideology is the practical *denegation* of the ideological character of ideology by ideology: ideology never says, 'I am ideological.'"[52]

No History

One might say that much of what had been said so far has been said already by Lukács. His entire theory after all is grounded on the problem of "class consciousness." What moves history for Lukács is not only material conditions but consciousness of the class-character of the values, ideas, and ideals that stabilize and reproduce the dominant order. Becoming conscious of the class-specific character of social forms enables dominated people to see through the universalist mystifications of the bourgeoisie, imagine a radically different society, and establish the actuality of that social order by revolution. But Althusser's theory is in detail radically different.

Althusser rejects Lukács's claim that the problem of ideology is exclusively a problem of thinking or "consciousness." Althusser holds that ideological thinking is chiefly a matter of the social *unconscious*. It functions in the form of an "imaginary relationship of individuals to their real conditions of existence."[53] Just as the Freudian unconscious underwrites imaginary experiences—dreams, fears, fantasies, and such—so too does ideology construct an imaginary relation between the individual and the real world. Althusser's reasoning here is worth noting.

Specific ideologies—religious, pedagogical, familial, etc.—have specific histories through which their content developed and changed. Therefore, Althusser notes, there "can be no question of a theory of ideolog*ies* in general" since no singular theory could meaningfully encompass the plurality of histories through which discrete ideologies formed.[54] But it is possible to give a general theory of ideology (in the singular) or what we could call the *ideological form*. But this commits him to a theory of ideology unbounded by any specific ideological content and thus any discrete history of its formation. His theory is a theory of ideology in general, not of historical ideologies. The theory is of necessity transhistorical. This he admits "entails an apparently paradoxical proposition which I shall express in the following terms: *ideology has no history*."[55] He looks to Freud for support. "To give a theoretical reference point here," writes Althusser, "our proposition: ideology has no history can and must ... be related directly to Freud's proposition that the *unconscious is eternal*, i.e., that it has no history."[56] Freud held that the content of the unconscious was historical because it formed through the experiences of the subject. But the unconscious itself as a psychic structure (or *form*) had no history. Althusser continues:

> If eternal means, not transcendent to all (temporal) history, but omnipresent, trans-historical and therefore immutable in *form* throughout the extent of history, I shall adopt Freud's expression word for word, and write ideology is eternal, exactly like the unconscious. And I add that I find this comparison theoretically

justified by the fact that the eternity of the unconscious is not unrelated to the eternity of ideology in general."[57]

The word "form" here does key work. Marx showed that it was possible to separate specific material histories from a general (or generalizable) form amenable to theorization. For example, Marx theorizes the *money form* as a distinct theoretical object apart from any specific monetary history. Likewise, Freud sought a theory of the unconscious as a form (or structure) as a distinct theoretical object separate from any specific individual's unconscious life. There are particular ideologies relayed by institutions and those have particular histories, but it makes no sense to speak of the history of ideology having forms. Ideology has always come in material forms. Althusser's transhistorical claim about ideology complexly interlinks with his claim about the State. We have to bear in mind that ideology for Althusser is always State ideology. But the State can't possibly be any singular State or any specific history of a State. Otherwise, the theory would be irreparably riven by the historicity of a specific State and the transhistorical character of the ideology form. The term "State" in the concept "Ideological State Apparatuses" must therefore be not an actual historical State but rather the *State form*.

Althusser theorizes ideology from the entwined perspective of the *ideology form* and that of the *State form*. Can one square Althusser's insistence on form (or even formalism) with his claim that he is in fact advancing a *materialist* theory of ideology? As Althusser notes with characteristic terseness, "*Thesis II: Ideology has a material existence.*"[58] He expands very little on this thesis. "Of course, the material existence of ideology in an apparatus and its practices," he writes, "does not have the same modality as the material existence of a paving stone or a rifle."[59] Ideology is material insofar as it is articulated in practices like teaching and preaching and in every form of subjection. "Of course, presented in affirmative form," the materialist claim for ideology, Althusser notes, "is ... unproven. I simply ask the reader be favorably disposed towards it, say, in the name of materialism. A long series of arguments would be necessary to prove it."[60] In "the name of materialism" is a call—following on from his arguments in "Lenin and Philosophy"—to get on the side of materialist philosophy in the ongoing battle against the forces of idealism. But if there is going to be a philosophy (or theory) of the materialist nature of ideology, then we would have to think through a theoretical unevenness: the materialist nature of the historically constituted ISAs and the transhistorical form of *ideology in general*. Of course, we can, as noted, separate general forms from historical formations. But that neat scission proves messy in the case of ideology. If we want to think the materialist nature of ideology—and separate that from the historicity of the materialist nature of its apparatuses—then we would have to formulate a theory of the *materiality of form*. The trouble is how to remain within a materialist problematic of the State and of ideology from the quasi-idealist vantage of the State form and the ideology form.[61] This problem also haunts the scene of interpellation to which we now turn.

Hey, You There!

The question of the possibility of a materialist theory of form haunts the most well-known concept advanced in the ISAs essay: *interpellation*. The arguments surrounding this concept are so well known that there has emerged a kind of fog of familiarity that today obscures some of the stranger aspects of this concept.

Althusser insists that "the category of the subject is constitutive of all ideology," but he adds that "*the category of the subject is only constitutive of all ideology insofar as ideology has the function (which defines it) of 'constituting' concrete individuals as subjects.*"[62] Of course, the "concrete individual" here is somewhat an obscure concept. It cannot mean the individual conceptualized by bourgeois philosophy. That is an ideological abstraction. By "concrete" he seems to mean a single human being who is capable of answering an interpellation or solicitation from the ISAs. The question is: how does a concrete individual become a good or bad subject from the standpoint of the ISAs? How does one become a subject? His answer takes the form of a descriptive "theoretical scene." He writes:

> I shall then suggest that ideology "acts" or "functions" in such a way that it "recruits" subjects among the individuals (it recruits them all), or "transforms" the individuals into subjects (transforms them all) by that very precise operation that I have called *interpellation* or hailing, and which be imagined along the lines of the most commonplace everyday police (or other) haling: "Hey, you there!"
>
> Assuming that the theoretical scene I have imagined takes place in the street, the hailed individual will turn round. By this mere one-hundred-and-eighty-degree physical conversion, he becomes a *subject*.[63]

By answering the call of State authority (in this case issued by the police), one becomes a subject in that one demonstrates physically that one has internally subjected oneself to State ideology. There is a profound tension between the descriptive and the general levels of the theory.

Specifically, the whole scene is presented temporally. But if the ideology form has no history and if ideology is constitutive of the subject, then one never becomes a subject: one is always-already a subject. This tension does not go unnoticed by Althusser. He writes:

> Naturally for the convenience and clarity of my little theoretical theater I have had to present things in the form of a sequence, with a before and an after, and thus in the form of temporal

succession. ... But in reality these things happen without any succession. The existence of ideology and the hailing or interpellation of individuals as subjects are one and the same thing.[64]

Ideological subjection is always-already an accomplished fact. There is no moment when one becomes a subject. Interpellation is not a call that concrete individuals answer one fine day. By the time the call of interpellation can even be *called a call*, it has been answered without ever having been answered to. The whole "theoretical theatre" of call and response is entirely inadequate to what is being articulated under the heading of "interpellation." We have to think a process that doesn't happen but has already-always happened. "As ideology is eternal," writes Althusser, "I must now suppress the temporal form in which I have presented the functioning of ideology and say ... *individuals are always-already subjects.*"[65]

The ISAs essay's theoretical saliency lies then in the way it might further thinking on what it means to live as always-already a subject and not only as a concrete individual. We would then have to reimagine the whole scene from Althusser's "theoretical theatre." The call of ideology—the cop in the street hailing someone—obscures Althusser's deeper point. The cop has already affirmed the hail of the State and so has the one who spins round thinking the cop's hailing was exclusively for him. The subject positions of cop and the subject who answers his call have already been assigned. Nothing new has happened in this scene. What has occurred is already a reproduction.

The Theory Form

Since ideology is an accomplished fact—and since one of the apparatuses that accomplishes that fact is teaching embodied in the ISA of the school—then it follows that Althusser's theory must be in some measure ideological. It cannot be that Althusser—a subject formed by his immersion in the academy and his position as the head of the philosophy department of the most elite university in France—is not also an ideological subject. Indeed, Althusser is explicit that we are all of us always-already subjects. Teaching and the institutions that embody it reproduce an ideology that subjectifies individuals and reproduces the authority of the State form. This should reframe how one reads Althusser's theoretical effort *or any theoretical effort*.

Any theory operationally affirms the always-already accomplished fact of an ideological capture: the established subject positions of teacher and student. In this minimal, but important, respect we could name this the State ideological dimension of theory: the *theory form*. Any social theory—*including any theory of ideology*—reproduces the *theory form*, which functionally affirms the always-already assigned positions of teacher and student even if these are represented simply in the forms of theoretical text (teacher) and reader (student). We will see in the next chapter that it is precisely this pedagogical ideology that Rancière will indict in *Althusser's Lesson*. Rancière there pushes this critique to its limits. He ends up indicting not only Althusser but any theory that presumes to teach dominated peoples the supposed secrets of their domination.

Althusser himself is not entirely blind to this issue. He too recognizes that the very positions of reader (student) and text (teacher) reproduce the ideology of the subject. He notes:

> In order to grasp what follows, it is essential to realize that both he who is writing these lines and the reader who reads them are themselves subjects, and therefore ideological subjects (a tautological proposition), i.e., that the author and the reader of these lines both live "spontaneously" or "naturally" in ideology.[66]

"Reader" and "author" are ideological subject positions which we live "spontaneously" or "naturally"—the positions of each subject both to the ideology of the subject or to ideology in general. The master is mastered by the pedagogical ideology just as the position of the student is. As Althusser declares, "[t]here are no subjects except by and for their subjection."[67] This means *to become a subject is to be subjected to the idea of the subject or the subject as such.* "We observe that the structure of all ideology," works, notes Althusser, by "interpellating individuals as subjects in the name of a Unique and Absolute Subject."[68] We are interpellated as students, teachers, theorists, militants, and so on by a speculative idea that we misrecognize as being "really" who we are. The subjects we become are only ever this Unique Subject or the Absolute Subject, which is at once an abstraction, a form, and the position from which we come to see ourselves as unique subjects. We are caught "in a double mirror-connection," the functioning of which "*subjects* the subjects to the Subject," notes Althusser, "while giving them in the Subject ... the *guarantee* that this really concerns them."[69] Ideology is a kind of alchemical process. The speculative (ideal) subject is materially realized in the misrecognition of the "I" as subject.

Ideology is the material reproduction of an idealist abstraction: *Subject-cum-subject*. This production process is circular. Every material result of the *subject-cum-subject* process reinstates the idealist abstraction of the Absolute Subject. Becoming a subject automatically reproduces the ideology of the subject or ideology in general.

Ideology Is Eternal

If ideology is eternal and immanent to the production of theory including every theory of ideology, then what is to be done? Specifically, what is theory (or the theorist) to do? In the chapters to follow we will see three possible models. For Rancière (Chapter 4), the problem of ideology is that of the politics of pedagogy. Ideology critique for him must suspend its presumed authority in the name of the knowledge of domination already articulated by dominated peoples. Radical thought worthy of the name must be rooted in the thought immanent to these struggles. It must also as a consequence destroy the foundations of theoreticism, which always-already signals the subjugation of thought to the division of intellectual and manual labor and therefore fundamentally to capital. Then, we will look to the work of Baudrillard (Chapter 5) in order to interrogate the question of what form theory might take in a conjuncture in which power solicits and subjectivizes us in the form of images, code, or "simulacra." Laruelle (Chapter 6) suggests a radical reversal of the problem set. It is a matter, for him, of taking the fight against ideology into the camp of philosophy itself. It is not a matter of constructing another (better) philosophy or theory of ideology but of axiomatizing the problem of the *ideology of philosophy*. It is a matter of tracing and resisting its modalities of intellectual despotism. Laruelle's "non-standard" philosophical imperative is to call out and dispel the command structure of philosophy's decisionism in the name of what is radically decisive in the last instance: *the real*.[70] I want then to trace some of the terrain opened by Althusser but left unexplored by him: that of the ideology of pedagogy and the figure of the pedagogue (Rancière); that of the object of theory (Baudrillard); and that of the ideology of philosophy (Laruelle).

Notes

1   Louis Althusser, "Reply to John Lewis," in *Essays in Self-Criticism*, 50.
2   Ibid., 51.
3   Ibid.
4   See E. P. Thompson, *The Poverty of Theory* (London: Monthly Review Press, 2008).

5   Roger Garaudy, *Marxism in the Twentieth Century*, trans. René Hague (New York: Charles Scribner's Sons, 1970), 205.
6   Jacques-Alain Miller, "Action of the Structure," in *Concept and Form: Volume One*, 70.
7   Ibid., 71.
8   Ibid.
9   Ibid., 74.
10 Ibid.
11 Ibid.
12 Ibid., 75.
13 Ibid., 70.
14 Louis Althusser, "On Cultural Revolution," trans. Jason Smith *Decalages* 1, no. 1 (2014): 3.
15 Ibid.
16 Ibid.
17 Ibid., 14.
18 Louis Althusser, *Philosophy and the Spontaneous Philosophy of the Scientists*, ed. Gregory Elliott, trans. Ben Brewster, et al. (London: Verso, 2011), 278.
19 Ibid., 278–9.
20 Mao Zedong, "On Practice," in *Selected Works of Mao Tse-Tung: Volume I* (Peking: Foreign Language Press, 1965), 297.
21 Ibid.
22 Ibid.
23 Louis Althusser, "Philosophy as a Revolutionary Weapon," in *Lenin and Philosophy and Other Essays*, trans. Ben Brewster (New York: Monthly Review Press, 2001), 8.
24 See Richard Wolin, *The Wind from the East: French Intellectuals, the Cultural Revolution, and the Legacy of the 1960s* (Princeton: Princeton University Press, 2017).
25 See Richard Wolin, *The Politics of Being: The Political Thought of Martin Heidegger* (New York: Columbia University Press, 1990).
26 See Walter Benjamin, "The Work of Art in the Age of Its Technological Reproducibility," in *The Work of Art in the Age of Its*

Technological Reproducibility and Other Writings on Media, ed. Michael W. Jennings, Brigid Doherty and Thomas Y. Levin, trans. Edmund Jephcott, Rodney Livingstone, Howard Eiland, and Others (Cambridge: Harvard University Press, 2008), 42.

27 See Laikwan Pang, *The Art of Cloning: Creative Production during China's Cultural Revolution* (London: Verso, 2010).
28 See Alexander C. Cook, ed. *Mao's Little Red Book: A Global History* (Cambridge: Cambridge University Press, 2014).
29 Pang, *The Art of Cloning*, 211.
30 Ibid.
31 Ibid., 206.
32 Ibid., 205.
33 Ibid., 201.
34 Louis Althusser, "Note on 'The Critique of the Personality Cult,'" in *Essays in Self-Criticism*, trans. Grahame Lock (London: NLB, 1976), 80.
35 Alain Badiou, *The Communist Hypothesis*, trans. David Macey and Steve Corcoran (London: Verso, 2010), 153.
36 Ibid., 154.
37 Pang, *The Art of Cloning*, 43.
38 Alain Badiou, *Theory of the Subject*, trans. Bruno Bosteels (London: Bloomsbury Academic, 2013), 7.
39 Tse-Tung, *On the Correct Handling of Contradictions among the People*, 31.
40 Louis Althusser, "Ideology and Ideological State Apparatuses: Notes toward an Investigation," in *Lenin and Philosophy and Other Essays*, trans. Ben Brewster (New York: Monthly Review Press, 2001), 89.
41 Ibid., 92.
42 Ibid.
43 Ibid.
44 Ibid., 93.
45 Ibid.
46 Ibid.
47 Ibid., 95.
48 Ibid., 107.

49 Ibid., 96.
50 Ibid., 98.
51 Marx and Engels, *The German Ideology*, 59.
52 Althusser, "Ideology and Ideological State Apparatuses," 118.
53 Ibid., 109.
54 Ibid., 107.
55 Ibid., 108.
56 Ibid., 109.
57 Ibid., italics mine.
58 Ibid., 112.
59 Ibid.
60 Ibid.
61 I owe a debt here to the work of Guillaume Sibertin-Blanc. His work on Deleuze and Guattari and their theory of the State helped me to better see this ideality of the State-form concept. See Guillaume Sibertin-Blanc, *State and Politics: Deleuze and Guattari on Marx*, trans. Ames Hodges (South Pasadena: Semiotext(e), 2016).
62 Althusser, "Ideology and Ideological State Apparatuses," 116.
63 Ibid., 118.
64 Ibid.
65 Ibid., 119.
66 Ibid., 116.
67 Ibid., 123.
68 Ibid., 122.
69 Ibid.
70 Note that in this text I have broken with Laruelle's convention of capitalizing "the real" as I think it can lead to confusion. The "real" is ordinary.

4

Rancière

In 1969, Rancière was teaching at Vincennes. This university was created in the summer of 1968 from the ashes of May. It attracted politically active students and faculty including Rancière and Badiou. Rancière wrote a short text in 1969 that was later published. "On the Theory of Ideology: Althusser's Politics" is based on a reading of Althusser's 1965 texts (the ISAs essay had not yet appeared). Rancière charges that the ideological dimension of Althusserianism lies in the way that it cuts itself off from political verification. It relies only on its immanent logical norms. "Theoretical practice contained its own norms of verification," writes Rancière.[1] Althusserian theory's autonomous reliance on its "own norms of verification" depended on nothing happening on the political front to call into question its theoretical correctness. Rancière writes:

> In May 1968, however, everything was suddenly and brutally clarified. As the class struggle broke out openly inside the university, the status of the "theoretical" was thrown into doubt, though not by the perennial blabber about praxis and the concrete but by the reality of a mass ideological revolt.[2]

May confronted Althusserianism with the theoretical problem of concrete class struggle. Althusserian theory's struggle against ideology is *allied* with the dominated classes. But the dominated, argues Rancière, do not determine intellectual direction of the struggle. This matter is left to professional scientists of Marxism-Leninism. Althusser's "exclusion of class struggle," writes Rancière, "prompts a particularly interesting game of theoretical hide-and-seek."³ Althusserianism teaches that dominated classes can and do combat ideology. But the nature and strategy of this combat is to be determined in advance by the intellectual class. Rancière concludes that Althusserianism amounts to a theoretical "elimination of class struggle."⁴ The elimination of actual class struggle from (early) Althusserianism is an ideology inasmuch as it does not recognize the *theoretical effects of concrete class struggle*. It thereby ratifies the existing "social whole." Althusserianism reproduces the ideology that science can be found only in theory and not in the immanent thought produced in and as struggle.

Lessons

Politically disappointed with (Althusserian) theory's response to May, Rancière turned to history. His dissertation project, *Nights of Labor*, later published as *Proletarian Nights*, lets the voices of nineteenth-century French workers speak for themselves rather than impose upon those voices party or theoretical edicts. He sought in this way to resist the division of labor reproduced by traditional Marxian theory: theorists theorize and intellectually lead workers who are there to do as they are told. Althusser's taught, according to Rancière, that workers lacked the scientific understanding of their conditions and needed intellectuals to show them the way out of the flytrap of ideology. Althusserianism secures "the power of those who arrogate to themselves the view of the master," writes Rancière, "over the historic process in which they declare others to be collectively enclosed."⁵ This "declaration of enclosure and this position of mastery," he continues, "found their radical form in the Althusserian enterprise in which I participated."⁶ Althusserian theory affirms the logic of capital: managers think up what workers must do.

Rancière argues that Althusser taught that workers "did not understand" the "laws of [their] domination" and that "they did not understand because they were dominated."[7] Althusserian theory therefore formed a "perfect circle" of logic.[8] It taught that "only scientists [of Marxism-Leninism]" who are "able to perceive the logic of this circle could lead them out of their subjection."[9] The lesson Rancière learned was that Althusserianism is effectively a pedagogy, an apparatus of interpellation, that hails or recruits cadres of theorists from elite classrooms. It teaches the virtues of a division of labor that accords to some the privilege of thought and to many the drudgery of work. As Ian James astutely notes:

> Rancière's charge [is] that Althusserian theory ... is fundamentally a theory of education ... As such, it preserves a structural inequality between the practitioners of the theory itself (who continue to enjoy the privileges of their university position) and the unenlightened masses in whose name Marxist theory is ostensibly practiced.[10]

The pedagogical effect of Althusserian theory keeps everyone in the place assigned to them by the dominant order. Althusserianism is an instance then of what Rancière will later term the order of the "police." Althusserian theory is an ideology that perpetuates the policing of the division between manual and intellectual work. Althusserianism presents ideology as an object of theory but not as a matter of practical-political struggle. "This lack of internal conflict or struggle within the constitution of ideology," writes James, "has the effect, Rancière contends, of naturalizing it and making it more or less a normal state of affairs."[11] Althusser's refusal to accord political and theoretical importance to May 1968 convinced Rancière that Althusserian science, a "science that claimed to explain subjection and guide revolt," was, writes Rancière, "complicit in the dominant order."[12] When revolt came, Althusserianism called for law and order: workers were to go back to work and students were to go back to class and await instructions from those who know best.

In 1971, Rancière offered, in lieu of a scheduled seminar on philosophy, a seminar devoted to archival research on labor and labor organizing in France in the early nineteenth century. The archives verified what had been demonstrated in the streets during May 1968. He learned again that dominated peoples "had never needed the secrets of domination explained to them."[13] Rancière found in the archives intellectual and political resources untapped by orthodox Marxist theory, the French Communist Party, and Althusser's seminar. Rancière's theoretical break was complete in 1974. That year he published *Althusser's Lesson*.

Althusser's Lesson charges Althusser with having ratified and reproduced the ideological division between mental and manual labor immanent to capitalism. This ideology rests on *the axiom of the inequality of intelligences*.[14] Althusserianism prizes the worker's material power to produce. But matters of thought are to be produced by those trained in Marxist science. This ideology preserves the dominant order. "The Marxism we learned from Althusser," notes Rancière, "was a philosophy of order."[15] Reflecting on *Althusser's Lesson* in 2010, Rancière notes: "My book declared war on the theory of the inequality of intelligences at the heart of supposed critiques of domination."[16] Althusserianism is presented as symptomatic of all theory that "declares the inability of the ignorant to be cured of their illusions," writes Rancière, and "the inability of the masses to take charge of their own destiny."[17] Rancière axiomatizes the inverse: "all revolutionary thought" must begin with the "inverse presupposition, that of the capacity of the dominated."[18] Let us turn briefly to the first chapter of *Althusser's Lesson* before turning to Rancière's study of nineteenth-century workers.

Rancière begins with Althusser's critique of John Lewis in the latter's essay: "Reply to John Lewis." Rancière criticizes Althusser for using the British Marxist, John Lewis, as a straw man against which Althusser marshals the full weight of "orthodox" Marxism-Leninism. Rancière notes with some humor:

> There was once a puzzled journalist, who could not understand why his desperate search for a photo of John Lewis for an article about the *Reply to John Lewis* had turned up nothing. This journalist, it seems safe to say, had not studied much philosophy. Otherwise he would have easily recognized in John Lewis that character ... generally known, quite simply, as common sense.[19]

"John Lewis" is an allegorical figure for the ideology of humanist commonsense against which Althusser fields the forces of Marxist-Leninist anti-humanism. "John Lewis" names all those who cling to the humanist ideology that history is made by humans. Marxism-Leninism (in the Althusserian voice) insists that masses in classes make history and *that* history is a *"process without a subject."*[20] "Reply to John Lewis" stages a war of position between "John Lewis" (as Marxism-humanism) and "M-L" (as Marxism-Leninism). Rancière writes:

> What does John Lewis say? "It is man [the human] who makes history." What does "M-L" say? "It is the masses which make history." As Althusser likes to say: everyone can see the difference. On one side, we have the thesis that the bourgeoisie tirelessly inculcate upon the incurable minds of the petite bourgeoisie [read intellectuals like John Lewis]; on the other, we have the scientific, proletarian thesis.[21]

Rancière charges that the scientificity of "Reply to John Lewis" is entirely staged. It is a theater of combat in which the determination of science and ideology is determined in advance by "orthodox" Marxist philosophy. "Althusser is speaking from *within philosophy,*" writes Rancière, "so that what he holds up for scrutiny are not conflicting analyses of concrete situations, but 'orthodox' and heterodox theses."²² The meaning of science is staged on the ground (or stage) of philosophy. Althusserianism determines the opposition between science and ideology on *philosophical grounds*. The philosophical identity of "orthodox" Marxist philosophy is determined tautologically by (and as) Althusserian theory.

Marxism-humanism (John Lewis) must be tried and convicted, argues Rancière, to preserve Althusser's "philosophy of order" and with it the ordering function of the division of labor. The lesson of "Reply to John Lewis" for workers is that they "should wait for the 'theses' that specialists in Marxism work out for their benefit."²³ What is being staged in "Reply to John Lewis," argues Rancière, is a counterrevolutionary ideology that found its concrete expression in Althusser's and the French Communist Party's "orthodox" response to May 1968: stand down and wait for instructions from those who know best. Rancière writes:

> The stakes are clear: preserve philosophy—"Marxist philosophy"—in particular as the exclusive business of academically trained specialists by upholding a division of labor that safeguards its place. This goal, diametrically opposed to Marx's, finds its way into theory through ... those who think for the masses and who develop theses for "scientific understanding." The hunt for humanist fireflies is the smokescreen that gives Althusser cover to restore the philosophical form of bourgeois philanthropy: *workers need our science.*²⁴

The very conjuncture in which Althusser published "Reply to John Lewis" had, in Rancière's view, already verified the inverse presupposition: the capacity of the dominated to take charge of their destiny. This axiom was verified by all who took to the streets in China, France, and Italy. "The moonlight that keeps Althusser awake," writes Rancière, "is that of the warm nights at Tsinghua University or the Sorbonne; of the thought that *workers don't need our science, but our revolt.*"²⁵

Les Révoltes Logiques

In 1975, Rancière founded the historical research journal, *Les Révoltes Logiques* [*Logical Revolts*]. The journal took its name from a line from Arthur Rimbaud's poem "Democracy." The poem is set, notes Oliver Davis, in the "emotional aftermath of the repression" of the Paris Commune of 1871 amidst "the dismantling or dimming of utopian conceptions of change."[26] The name of the journal twists to the Left the reactionary voice that speaks in Rimbaud's poem: "We shall massacre the logical revolts."[27] Against the imperious reign of the poem's voice—a voice of reactionary restoration and "law and order"—the journal sought "to salvage and restore the memory of past revolts," writes Davis, "by contrast with an official history which had consigned them to the unpromising category of 'failures.'"[28]

The name of the journal performed in word what the journal sought to do in deed: resist the marginalization of revolt by Left and Right historiography alike. It sought to perform a "torsion" of the historiographic bias against revolt; to wrench it back from the melancholic disappointment of the Left for which revolts are failed revolutions, and from the epistemic violence of the Right, which seeks to efface or "massacre" the memory of revolts and thereby neutralize the possibility of alternative and radical futures.[29] The project's name also resonated with the then popular Maoist slogan: "It is right to rebel." Rancière was sympathetic to Maoism at the time. But his sympathy was ambivalent. In an early article for the journal, Rancière reflects on research that would in time culminate with the publication of *Proletarian Nights*:

> My first intention was to track down the initial identity of the specific thinking of the working class that the overlay of Marxist discourse had covered up. I had been involved in a movement that maintained that all the ideas of Marxism could be summed up in

a single one: "It is right to rebel." Unfortunately, this movement soon exhausted itself in trying to give the pure negativity of this subjectless assertion the face of proletarian positivity, and discovered that the reasons for rebellion were rather more complex than they appeared at first sight. It seemed necessary then, in order to understand the wall that had arisen between empirical proletarians and the proletarian discourse we had lent them, to go back to the point of origin at which Marxist discourse first came to graft itself onto the voices of working-class protest.[30]

Les Révoltes Logiques sought to illuminate the political logics of past revolts by stripping their historical record clean of bourgeois and orthodox Marxist overlays—an effort that resonated with an entire generation of Western Marxists, in France, Italy, and elsewhere, who were committed to the overthrow of capital and the dogma of the official Left parties. The journal, as Davis notes, emphasized the "logic" of revolts by privileging their "critical, analytical, and linguistic dimensions."[31] "Thus 'logiques' reflects less the inexorability of spontaneous resistance," writes Davis, "and points to the words, the language involved in that resistance."[32]

Rancière's concern for language is clear in *Proletarian Nights*. Workers' language (or logic) is treated as part of the material of revolt and not merely its expression. What "is known as revolt," writes Rancière, "is also a scene of speech and reasons: it is neither the eruption of popular savagery which escapes the disciplinary effects of power ... nor is it the expression of historical necessity and legitimacy."[33] Revolt is neither, as the Right have it, a primal expression of "savagery," nor is it evidence for the Leftist version of transcendental historiography according to which revolt is simultaneously a failed revolution *and* the messianic promise of revolution yet to come. The project sought to extricate the historical logic of revolts *and to catalyze a logical revolt against traditional working-class historiography*.

To Work

Proletarian Nights stages the capitalist interpellative imperative *to work* against the backdrop of proletarian nightlife—the dreamtime of aesthetic and philosophic production—forms of work that did not count as work because they were unwaged. Workers' aesthetic and philosophic work disturbed the social order according to which workers work, artists create, philosophers think, and the bosses rule. Intellectual and aesthetic production by workers sometimes took form in verse, image, and written thought. But it also took the oneiric form of daydreaming. These forms of work verified that the established division of labor "was arbitrary and therefore changeable."[34] "This demonstration was," notes Davis, "simultaneously both political and aesthetic."[35] Workers' intellectual and aesthetic work challenged the norm of specialization enshrined by the capitalist division of labor. It verified the capacity of the dominated to rupture the "common sense" (ideological) division between manual and mental labor.

Proletarian Nights is made up of a set of case studies drawn from the margins of the mass industrialized workforce. They are artisans, the semi-employed, the precariously employed, and the unemployed. They dream not of a worker's paradise but of "another kind of work."[36] Indicative is the case of the locksmith J.-P. Gilland who notes: "I would like to have been a painter. But poverty enjoys no privileges, not even that of choosing this or that fatigue for a living."[37] How to historically account for this dream of another kind of work, the dream of indeed choosing the form of one's fatigue? And how would reigning ideologies of Marxist historiography have to change to accommodate this dreamtime? "What is at stake here is not the right to idleness but the dream of another kind of work," writes Rancière, "that is a gentle movement of the hand, slowly following the eyes, on a polished surface."[38] It is a dream of "producing something other," writes Rancière, "than the wrought objects in which the philosophy of the future [communism and capitalism alike] sees the essence of man-the-producer being realized."[39]

Proletarian Nights tells the story of how intellectual factions—across the reformist-revolutionary spectrum—vied for the allegiance of the working class. Rancière suggests that when their interpellative efforts failed, they did because they failed to register workers' *ambivalence* with the very idea of waged work. The case studies demonstrate, notes Donald Reid, that "relatively unskilled workers deeply ambivalent about manual labor had played prominent roles in the workers' movement."[40] Telling is this quotation from Gilland taken from an article he wrote for *La Ruche populaire*:

> It seems to me that I have not found my vocation in hammering iron, although there is nothing ignoble about that calling. Far from it! From the anvil comes the warrior's sword that defends the liberty of peoples and the plowshare that feeds them. Great artists have caught the ample, manly poetry of our bronzed faces and our robust limbs, rendering it with great felicity and energy.[41]

Gilland's identification with work is ambivalent. He writes that "hammering iron" is not his "vocation" or calling. But this is followed by a celebration of manual labor as essential to life (plowshares) and liberty (swords). Gilland underscores its importance by noting that labor has been (and can be) the subject of art. But, as noted, Gilland later admits: "I would have liked to have been a painter. But poverty enjoys no privileges, not even that of choosing this or that fatigue for a living."[42] It is this "dream" of not only being a cultural producer but also the dream of emancipation from the iron laws of necessity that Rancière reads as voiced resistance to the interpellative call *to work*.

The historical privilege that Rancière pays to "night" is key. It signals his temporal orientation against the then prevailing fashion to spatialize historical thought. Kristin Ross argues that

Rancière opposed theoretical trends of the day typified by the work of thinkers such as Michel Foucault, Fredric Jameson, and Gilles Deleuze among others.[43] Ross notes that at the time Rancière's first major historiographic works appeared "the interdisciplinary terrain had begun to be taken over and inundated ... with a kind of cobbled-together 'spatiality,' as the human sciences came to embrace insights, perspectives, and methodologies imported from the 'spatial sciences' of urbanism, architecture, ethnology, and geography."[44] According to Ross, these disciplines constructed "the category of culture as a static, spatial countenance—culture that cannot be seen as an agent of time."[45] The spatializing concept of culture harbors a political conservatism. It privileges smooth historical space and elides evental ruptures. The spatial turn still has effects. Today, notes Ross, scholars tend to "shy away from large diachronic questions and from any attempt to conceptualize change, preferring instead to nest [it] within a set of spatially determined cultural units of comparison."[46] The space of comparison on the terrain of spatiality forces any conception of history "outside" the temporality of evental historicity. The writing of history in this vein becomes an alibi for the status quo.

Rancière's writings historicize worker-led intellectual resistance in its actual and oneiric forms. This was a dream to take possession of the means of intellectual and aesthetic production. It was a dream not merely to be the object of art and thought but the dream of "moving to the other side of the canvas."[47] It was also the dream of a free relation to art. "I could not help but stop and go into ecstasy before the shops with pictures and engravings," notes Gilland in a letter to Georges Sand.[48] This ecstasy of aesthetic enjoyment is the dream of enjoyment emancipated from commodification. Gilland's gaze appropriates the commodified art in the shop window for free—an instance perhaps of what Rancière will later term the "emancipated spectator."[49]

Empirical Proletarians

Plato infamously called for the exclusion of artists from his ideal State. This exclusion became in the nineteenth century the ideology of "art-for-art's-sake." A case in point is Alphonse Viollet. Rancière quotes his description of an anonymous tailor poet. "In his long breaks he took special delight in executing little products of fantasy that were good for nothing."[50] Viollet inscribes his subject's identity within the frame of waged (useful) work. Waged work is the primary identity through which the anonymous producer is read back into the capitalist frame that his "useless" labor actually resists. The dream of autonomy and sovereignty—the dream of being a free maker—is held in check by Viollet's modernist sensibility that grants to art (not to persons) autonomy. What is telegraphed by Gilland's articulation of his dream and that of the anonymous tailor is the dream not of useless and gloriously autonomous aesthetic objects but of "another kind of work" emancipated from the wage form.

Workers against work is a consistent thematic of *Proletarian Nights*. Consider Cailloux who apprenticed as a joiner. He later quit. He wound up selling in the marketplace knickknacks for "fifteen to twenty sous".[51] Cailloux's apprenticeship was an interpellative failure. It failed to *make him into a joiner*. "I never took a liking to the work," notes Cailloux, "for the simple reason that I had been overwhelmed by it and [it] never [held the] the least enjoyment [for me]."[52] Cailloux's experience—his failure to become a professional joiner—drove him into precarity. His figure drops out of the records from which the imaginaries of working-class historiography are traditionally composed. Rancière's historiography follows the logic of Cailloux's trajectory. It moves beyond the confines and sureties of the idealist political historiography of the proletariat. It follows the path trod by "empirical proletarians."[53] Rancière writes:

> [T]his aleatory population, in every sense of the word, represents less the army of the marginal or declassed than the proletariat

in its very essence that is concealed under the wretched or glorious images of the factory damned .... They represent very accurately the aleatory history and geography that bring together those individuals who live, each and every one, in the absolute precariousness of having no trump to play but the availability of their arms and suffering from the day-to-day uncertainty of their employment more than from the exploitation of their product.[54]

Proletarians like Cailloux did not identify with forms of work. They identified with the problem of looking for and securing work. As the chairmaker, Dagoreau, noted to a Saint-Simonian organizer: "I would remind you that no sort of work in line with my physical and moral powers ... is repugnant to me. ... If need be, I could wear the blouse, short jacket, and cap ... or don a broadcloth coat and pants."[55] Types of work for workers like Dagoreau were as interchangeable (and forgettable) as changes of clothes.

Proletarian Nights charts the aleatory path trod by workers in and out of work and in and out of political organizations. Consider the case of seamstress Désirée Véret. One Sunday she went to a Saint-Simonian meeting to, she notes, "find a bit of droll amusement."[56] But she left the meeting "filled with admiration for the grandeur of the ideas."[57] Véret's experience is a case of interpellative failure by the Saint-Simonians. She was compelled but not in the way they hoped. She does not become an "apostle" of the movement. She became instead an emancipated spectator. Rancière asks:

> What relationship is there between the Sunday extravagances ... and the solid realities of exploitation and class struggle? As with every other vertigo and every Sunday, it is one of everything and nothing. Monday will begin again the monotony of work or the vagrancy of unemployment. The world remains unchanged when the young seamstress leaves the Saint-Simonians preaching session ... Nothing has changed, but nothing will ever be the same as before either.[58]

Véret's interpellative refusal opens a space external to both the Saint-Simonian organizers and the bourgeois defenders of poverty. Both interpellative calls failed to recruit her. She neither becomes an "apostle" of the Saint-Simonians nor is she ignorant of her domination. Véret's subject position has slipped two interpellative traps: the call *to work* issued by the bourgeoisie and the work-centric politics of the reformists.

To what extent are figures like Véret, Cailloux, or Gilland representative of a larger movement in history and to what extent did they institute actual political change?[59] Is Rancière suggesting, asks Davis, "that later political insurrections were caused, at least in part, by nocturnal versifiers?"[60] Were the mass revolts and insurrections of the 1840s and 1871 prepared for in advance by workers who had sought their dignity and autonomy through intellectual and aesthetic production in the 1830s? Yes, this indeed seems to be his point. The insurrections were logically prepared for in advance by workers who refused the interpellative call *to work*. The insurrections were strikes not against working conditions alone. They were militant offensives against the very idea of waged work.

Proletarian Nights stages a logical revolt against the logic of standard political historiography in which "revolt" is defined only as a spectacular instance of insurrectionary violence and instead indexes the political saliency of silent refusal. The novelty of Rancière's historiography is not that he rejects the simplistic concept of class as economic in the last instance. Indeed, that is something that his work shares with much Marxist historiography of the period. What is novel is that Rancière takes seriously that the working class (in part) was and is a *class against waged work*. This aspect of Rancière's work aligns his project with autonomous Marxist movements then on the move in Italy. It is to this that I turn in order to trace this *sub-rosa* connection. There is also a methodological parallel to note as well: *co-research*. The diverse autonomous movements were galvanized by the principle of co-research conducted by members of the intellectual and working class inquiring together. This principle was also a political intervention to counter the ideological effects of the division of labor, which reproduces the divide between thought and action. Autonomous movements in Italy practiced in some measure what Rancière's post-Althusserian theoretical production sought to conceptually enact: a practice that verifies that working-class peoples are capable of leadership on the intellectual, cultural, and political fronts.

Autonomy

The 1950s was a time of industrial resurgence in Italy. The so-called economic miracle spurred a great migration from the agrarian south to the industrialized north. Yet despite the infusion of new workers into the industrial cities, enrollment in the Socialist Party of Italy (PSI) and Communist Party of Italy (PCI) fell dramatically. The reformist tendency of the Left parties failed to inspire and radicalize new workers. Indicative of the mood is the following recollection by a worker at the automaker, Fiat. The worker below recounts his impression of a visit from Palmiro Togliatti (then leader of the PCI) and Alcide de Gasperi (founder of the right-wing Christian Democrats):

> I remember ... [when] Togliatti came to speak ... and then De Gasperi came—and they both argued exactly the same thing; the need to save the economy ... We've got to work hard because Italy's on her knees ... but don't worry because if we work hard, in a year or two we'll all be fine.[61]

The worker's statement exemplifies the frustration felt by a generation of workers who were abandoned to the consensus of the center.

The established Left parties traded their founding revolutionary orientations for electoral respectability. This created a vacuum in genuine Left leadership into which stepped intellectuals and activists such as Mario Tronti, Antonio Negri, Raniero Panzieri, Romano Alquati, and others. The broad movement, known as *operaismo* or "workerism," was represented by political groups such as Potere Operaio (Workers' Power) and by journals such as *Quaderni Rossi* (*Red Notebooks*) and *Classe Operaia* (*Working Class*).

These more centralized theoretical and political efforts eventually morphed into a decentralized network of autonomous groups, which included Autonomia Operaia (Workers' Autonomy).

These organizations pushed for the intellectual and political autonomy of the working class without sanction or censure by Marxist academicians, the trade unions, or the leadership of the Left parties.

There were many internal splits and external rivalries between autonomous groups. But they shared much too. They took seriously that the working class had to be reimagined politically in a way that reflected the new class composition imposed by changes in the conditions of work wrought by automation and class diversification. Shibboleths regarding the supposed historical mission of the industrial working class were thrown out. Emblematic of the new spirit are the essays comprising Tronti's *Workers and Capital*. In "What the Proletariat Is," Tronti argues that changes in factory work, such as the use of the so-called gradings ladder for workers, diluted the effectiveness of traditional trade unionist strategies. The gains won by workers for better pay and hours had further incorporated them into the machinery of value production. The new struggle, the autonomists argued, had to be oriented toward the abolition of work and with it the proletarian class. "The proletariat … is compelled as proletariat," writes Tronti, "to abolish itself and thereby its opposite, private property, which determines its existence and which makes it proletariat."[62]

Workerism prizes the right of the working class to autonomously lead the intellectual and political struggles against capital. Years later, Tronti reflected on what about workerism for him remains vital. His comments succinctly summarize the workerist perspective.

> Some things remain ... the partisan point of view from which to address everything—that remains; the conflictual conception of the social relationship—that remains; the subjectivity of struggles ... that remains. But what remains for me above all is the political reading of the class struggle, the anti-economicism, the anti-sociologism, the anti-ideologism.[63]

Workerism (and autonomist strains of Marxism broadly) contrasts sharply with traditional Marxian theory's privileging of science. Tronti notes: "I am not looking for ... truth that is objective and good for all inorganic intellectuals. I am looking for a forceful political idea, which I need in order to build a battlefront that goes to the root of the current social divisions."[64]

Theoretical investigation is only *politically* useful, Tronti argues, if it can penetrate to the core of the system to struggle with workers in combat against capitalism. Workerism hold that the duty of the organic intellectual is first to learn from the working class and then to battle with the working class. Tronti writes:

> Analyzing the forms of struggle is an important passage in reconstructing the working-class point of view we seek, and it will be necessary to insist on this analysis in the future with particular studies. Once we resolve the problem of what workers set forward as their purpose, it is necessary to understand what the working class is; this is not possible without seeing how it struggles.[65]

A new relation between theory and practice thus emerged in which the practice of co-research—conducted between the intellectual and the working classes—served in practice as a theoretical countermodel to traditional party-theoretical vanguardism.

The practice of co-research or "workers' inquiry" was among the first signs of innovation in the earliest expressions of autonomous Marxism. As early as 1959, in the pages of *Quaderni Rossi*, there appeared a study of current conditions within Fiat. Signed by Alquati, "The Report on the New Forces" drew "primarily upon interviews with Fiat workers hired since the late 1950s."[66] Steve Wright, in his invaluable study, notes that "The Report" was an example of the political promise of co-research. Even if "The Report" was "somewhat impressionistic and rudimentary," notes Wright, it nonetheless "registered problems undetected by the leadership of the traditional left."[67] The major union, Italian General Confederation of Labor (CGIL), and the Left parties were, in Alquati's view, so out of touch with changing working conditions that it was "enough to describe it" in "everyday language to produce a work of political and cultural interest."[68] "The Report" surfaced at a moment when Fiat was attempting to pull off a corporate image makeover. "In these years, FIAT met with a certain success in projecting a new identity of high wages, valuable skills and dynamic career structures," notes Wright, "to overshadow its traditional reputation as a ruthless employer."[69] "The Report" punctured the veneer of the new and improved Fiat. It evaluated the firm on the basis of its actual treatment of workers. "The Report" showed that the firm's new policies were strategically designed to intensify divisions between workers. Wright notes:

> The first task of "co-research" was to strip bare the public myths attached to FIAT, and this the group accomplished with consummate skill. The much-vaunted "FIAT wage" was shown to now lag behind many other Italian firms. It was also revealed that, far from acquiring new skills, most of the workers taken on since 1958 were in the bottom category of the gradings ladder, many of them working as "common labor" on the assembly line. Finally, it was established that the prospects of a "career" promised to a new generation of firm-trained technical workers simply did not

exist. This, Alquati argued, was proof that the system of gradings which separated the great unwashed of the common laborers from the skilled workers and technicians did not have any basis at all in the "objective" technical division of labor; instead, its function was fundamentally political, operating to make employees accept the existence of hierarchies within and without the factory as a natural fact.[70]

The division of labor into segmented hierarchies on the factory floor reproduced and naturalized the very idea of hierarchic authority, which worked to politically divide workers against each other. Its purpose served not the ends of production but the ideological structuring necessary for the reproduction of production.

Co-research projects like "The Report" also revealed that industrial conditions now extended well beyond the factory gates. The use of scientific assessments of efficiency and viability, for example, became hegemonic in the management of nonindustrial work and social life as a whole. Thus, at the very moment when bourgeois economists were theorizing the emergence of a "postindustrial" epoch, the industrialization of nonindustrial production was actually ramping up. Autonomists came to the conclusion that society itself was being turned into a *social factory*.[71] As Tronti notes, "the factory extends its control over the whole society—all of social production is turned into industrial production."[72] The working class was no longer concentrated in factories alone. It was becoming increasingly dispersed into the social fabric through a host of non-unionized, casualized, service jobs. The saliency of trade unionism decreased as the ranks of the casualized sector increased. The autonomous movements responded to this change in class composition by focusing resistance on the conditions for the reproduction of work: housing, sexual reproduction, food, transportation, education, and the mass media and communications industries. Above all, they centered their political energies on the resistance to work itself.

Strikes, demands for better wages, and working conditions are important, but, autonomists argue, these also prolong capital's ability to adapt to changing working conditions. "Capitalist power seeks to use the workers' antagonistic will-to-struggle," notes Tronti, "as a motor of its own development."[73] Clarifying the distinction between the concept of the strike and that of refusal, Tronti notes that "[s]topping work does not in fact mark a refusal to *give* capital the use of one's labor-power ... since it has already been given to capital through the legal contract stipulating the sale and purchase of this particular commodity."[74] The autonomists of the late 1960s and 1970s focused on the intensification of the struggle for the emancipation of the whole of society from domination by the industrializing imperative. Tronti writes of the necessity for a "new form of antagonism."[75] He writes:

> The form of this struggle is the refusal, the organization of the working-class "No": the refusal to collaborate actively in capitalist development, the refusal to put forward a positive programme of demands. We can identify the germ of these forms of struggle and organization right from the very start of the working-class history of capital, right from the time that the first proletarians were constituted as a class. But the full development, the real significance of these forms comes much later, and they still exist as a strategy for the future.[76]

Key to this new strategy of refusal was political affectivity. The autonomists theoretically and practically reclaimed the affectivity of indifference, boredom, and passivity as political expressions of a latent desire to refuse work not merely to improve it. This concern with affect manifested in a number of creative practices that were central to the autonomous movements. The work of Nanni Balestrini is exemplary. It is to his work that I turn for a moment to explore this affective dimension.

Work Is Shit

Balestrini's 1971 novel, *We Want Everything*, is about an anonymous worker from southern Italy who goes north to Turin to take up work in a Fiat factory. The worker's political radicalization begins with a mix of disinterest and disgust with work in general. He says:

> I've done all kinds of work, bricklayer, dishwasher, loading and unloading. I've done it all, but the most disgusting is Fiat. When I came to Fiat I believed I'd be saved. ... In reality it's shit, like all work, in fact it's worse. Every day here they speed up the line. A lot of work and not much money. Here, little by little, you die without noticing. Which means that it's work that is shit, all jobs are shit.[77]

The worker begins to get involved in work stoppages and strikes mostly because these activities are preferable to the dull continuity of the daily grind. One day, he hears a work stoppage taking place on the far side of the factory. He goes over to see what is going on.

> The body workshops are huge sheds, so big you can't hear human speech. The workers have to shout to be heard. I heard trouble, shouting, and I said to myself: It's the comrades starting a demonstration. ... I abandon my post ... and I go to the comrades. I get there and I join in the shouting, too. We were shouting the strangest things, things that had fuck-all to do with anything, to create a moment of rupture: Mao Tsetung, Ho Chi Minh, Potere operaio. Things that had no connection to anything there but that we liked the sound of.[78]

This fictive scene articulates the very real feeling of political joy induced by an aesthetic practice of voicing in which what is enunciated attains a momentary autonomy from the logic, positionality, and empirical site of the workplace.

Balestrini reminds us that creativity and affect are integral to the impassioned politics of commitment. But much of anti-capitalist writing is rational and dispassionate. This tendency to an extent reproduces the cold and dispassionate affectivity of capital. When "reason" (*qua* economic rationality) is the pilot light of radical political economy, it risks blinding itself to the affective forms through which political struggles are articulated. This mode of analysis can also turn into an intellectual paternalism that treats workers' feelings as naive sentiments that are best ignored in favor of scientific analysis. The demand for scientificity in all things political can stifle the power of political affectivity and lead precisely to the cul-de-sac of the division of labor between thought and action as noted by Rancière.

Political vocabularies are not neutral. They are sites through which class is politically made and unmade, signified, and re-signified within and through struggle. Words like classes are defined through social processes. Meaning in both cases is made. E. P. Thompson was therefore absolutely correct when he noted that "class happens."[79] Thompson, like Rancière, argues against restrictive economistic notions of class and for an understanding of class as a cultural and, above all, a political notion. Thompson writes in *The Making of the English Working Class*:

> The making of the working class is a fact of political and cultural, as much as economic history. It was not the spontaneous generation of the factory-system. Nor should we think of an external force—the force of the "industrial revolution"—working upon some nondescript undifferentiated raw material of humanity, and turning it out at the other end as a "fresh race of human beings."[80]

Thompson correctly sees that class happens through political and cultural practice. But he sometimes misses the connection between the two. Consider the following:

> As the effect of ... [mass] school[ing] increasingly became felt, as well as the drive for self-improvement among working people themselves, so the number of the illiterate fell ... But the ability

to read was only the elementary technique. The ability to handle abstract and consecutive argument was by no means inborn; it had to be discovered against almost overwhelming difficulties—the lack of leisure, the cost of candles (or spectacles), as well as educational deprivation. Ideas and terms were sometimes employed in the early Radical movement ... [in a] ... fetishistic [way] rather than [a] rational ... [way]. Some of the Pentridge rebels [for example] thought that a "Provisional Government" would ensure a more plentiful supply of "provisions;" while in one account of the pitmen of the north-east in 1819, "Universal Suffrage" is understood by many of them to mean universal suffering ... 'if one member suffers, all must "suffer."'[81]

Thompson humorously notes the workers' resignification of "provisional government" and "universal suffrage," but he does not grasp its political implications. These semantic torsions are instances (intentional or not) of poetic-political resignification in Rancière's sense. Why can't Thompson hear what the workers say? *We want a government that will provide provisions for the people. We want an ethics of compassion for which the suffering of one is the suffering of all.* These semantic torsions are neither solely poetic nor simply political in nature; they are also philosophical. To conceptualize an alternative society in the form of "abstract and consecutive argument" requires first envisioning another possible society, the contours of which can be imagined through the raw material of existing vocabularies. Lest we forget: first came *The Communist Manifesto* and then the "abstract and consecutive argument" contained in *Capital*.

Co-research with the Dead

One might object that the movements associated with Italian autonomous Marxism were coordinated and militant movements whereas *Proletarian Nights* is focused upon singular and personal accounts of nineteenth-century workers. But we need to differentiate the individual scenes collected in *Proletarian Nights* from what Félix Guattari might call the text's *collective assemblage of enunciation*. Rancière's logic parallels the political convictions of the autonomous movements in its affirmation of the political and intellectual autonomy of workers; in its political reclamation of passivity, boredom, and indifference; in the significance accorded to aesthetic and philosophical production; and in its political prioritization of all that has "fuck-all" to do with work.

The archives taught Rancière the power and intelligence embodied in workers who refused the interpellative call of work and work-centric politics. For the French workers of the 1830s as for the autonomists the problem was the same: the social conditions that make the problem of work paramount in the first place. Their response was, to quote Rancière, "to withdraw themselves, intellectually and materially, from the forms by which this domination [by work] imprinted, and imposed on their actions, modes of perception, attitudes and language."[82] Such workers embodied the oneiric possibility that the world might be otherwise. Rancière writes:

> For the workers of the 1830s, the question was not to demand the impossible, but to realize it themselves, to take back the time that was refused them by educating their perceptions and their thought in order to free themselves in the very exercise of everyday work, or by winning from nightly rest the time to discuss, write, compose verses, or develop philosophies. These gains in time and freedom were not marginal phenomena or diversions in relation to the construction of the workers' movement and its great objectives. They were the revolution, both discreet and radical, that made these possible, the work by which men and women wrenched themselves out of an identity formed by domination and asserted themselves as inhabitants with full rights of a common world, capable of all refinement or all asceticism that had previously been reserved for those classes relieved of the daily cares of work and bread.[83]

Rancière's point resonates with one of the most important slogans of the Italian autonomous movements: "Demand nothing; take everything!" The French workers of the 1830s refused to ask or demand anything. Their revolt as for the autonomists was one of radical refusal: the refusal of work and of the division between intellectual and manual labor which securitizes and polices workers' intellectual and political powers. They rejected the trade unionist concept and strategy of "demand" for it reproduces and naturalizes the labor/managerial hierarchy. The concept and strategy of the "demand" depend upon and reproduce the axiom of inequality that structures and secures the intellectual's place in capitalist society.

Rancière, like the workerist intellectuals, learned to learn from workers. Both learned from work refusers a form of revolt that was both "discrete and radical" through which workers "wrenched themselves out of an identity formed by domination." These workers realized a subjectivation resistant to the identity imposed by the logic and politics of waged work.

Proletarian Nights is a political intervention. Its highly selective case studies are calculated to provoke a scientific demand for more evidence. But the book refuses the demand for a historians' history of the French working class. It answers a political demand not for historical science but for logical revolt. It hails the reader to refuse the interpellative call of orthodox Marxist theory. It solicits the reader to learn from those workers who answered the ideology of authority and that of the authorities on ideology with the revolt of radical refusal.

Rancière's turn from theory to the history of "empirical proletarians" represents a decisive break with Althusser. He came to embrace as revolutionary an "empiricist" conception of historical knowledge gleaned from the testimonial archive of working-class protest. His turn from theoreticism to historicism was not to last. His later work—especially on aesthetics and politics—turns back to theory if only in the form of a critique of what he still sees as the reactionary assumptions of intellectual vanguardism. But the work of both periods—his historical studies and his aesthetic theory—continues in a *sub rosa* sense a critique of the subject. Rancière's valorization of the archive of working-class protest and the archive of aesthetic history attempts to dispel the subject of theory embodied in the reactionary form of intellectual aristocratism and the division of intellectual and manual labor that secures its privileges. The next chapter examines the work of Baudrillard. His work also calls into question the emancipatory claims of critical theory especially its attempt to dispel the subject. This effort he sees as complicit in its reanimation. His solution will not be to once again renew the critique of the subject but to turn to the matter of the object.

Notes

1 Jacques Rancière, *Althusser's Lesson*, trans. Emiliano Battista (London: Bloomsbury Academic, 2011), 129.
2 Ibid.
3 Ibid., 135.
4 Ibid., 137.
5 Jacques Rancière, *Proletarian Nights: The Workers' Dream in Nineteenth-Century France*, trans. John Drury (New York: Verso), viii.
6 Ibid.
7 Ibid.
8 Ibid.
9 Ibid., viii–ix.
10 Ian James, *The New French Philosophy* (Cambridge: Polity Press, 2012), 115.
11 Ibid., 116.
12 Rancière, *Proletarian Nights*, ix.
13 Ibid.
14 A key idea in Rancière's later writings.

15 Rancière, *Althusser's Lesson*, xix.
16 Ibid., xvi.
17 Ibid.
18 Ibid.
19 Ibid., 1.
20 Althusser, *Essays in Self-Criticism* 51.
21 Rancière, *Althusser's Lesson*, 2.
22 Ibid.
23 Ibid., 10.
24 Ibid., 11-12.
25 Ibid., 12.
26 Kristin Ross quoted in Oliver Davis, *Jacques Rancière* (Cambridge: Polity Press), 39.
27 Davis, *Jacques Rancière*, 39.
28 Ibid.
29 Ibid.
30 Jacques Rancière, *Staging the People: The Proletarian and His Double*, trans. David Fernbach (New York: Verso, 2011), 21-2.
31 Davis, *Jacques Rancière*, 39.
32 Ibid., 39-40.
33 Quoted in Ibid., 40.
34 Davis, *Jacques Rancière*, 53.
35 Ibid.
36 Quoted in Rancière, *Proletarian Nights*, 8.
37 Ibid.
38 Rancière, *Proletarian Nights*, 8.
39 Ibid.
40 Donald Reid, "Introduction," *Proletarian Nights*, xxii-xxiii.
41 Quoted in Rancière, *Proletarian Nights*, 4.
42 Ibid., 8.
43 See Kristin Ross, "Historicizing Untimeliness," in *Jacques Rancière: History, Politics, Aesthetics*, ed. Gabriel Rockhill and Philip Watts (Durham: Duke University Press, 2009).
44 Ross, "Historicizing Untimeliness," 17.

45 Ibid.
46 Ibid.
47 Rancière, *Proletarian Nights*, 5.
48 Quoted in Ibid., 6.
49 See Jacques Rancière, *The Emancipated Spectator*, trans. Gregory Elliott (New York: Verso, 2011).
50 Quoted in *Proletarian Nights*, 8.
51 Ibid., 148.
52 Ibid.
53 Rancière, *Proletarian Nights*, 220.
54 Ibid., 147.
55 Quoted in Ibid., 155.
56 Ibid., 19.
57 Ibid.
58 Rancière, *Proletarian Nights*, 19.
59 Davis, *Jacques Rancière*, 53.
60 Ibid., 54.
61 Quoted in Steve Wright, *Storming Heaven: Class Composition and Struggle in Italian Autonomous Marxism* (London: Pluto Press, 2017), 8.
62 Mario Tronti, *Workers and Capital*, trans. David Broder (New York: Verso, 2019), 184–5.
63 Quoted in Antonio Negri, *Marx in Movement: Operaismo in Context*, trans. Ed Emery (Cambridge: Polity Press, 2022), 154.
64 Quoted in Ibid., 154.
65 Quoted in Ibid., 198.
66 Wright, *Storming Heaven*, 42.
67 Ibid.
68 Quoted in Ibid., 42.
69 Wright, *Storming Heaven*, 43.
70 Ibid., 43–4.
71 Here I think it should be noted that this was precisely the conclusion reached by Adorno and Horkheimer concerning the culture industry. See Theodor W. Adorno and Max Horkheimer, *Dialectic of Enlightenment: Philosophical Fragments*, ed. Gunzellin Schmid Noerr, trans. Edmund Jephcott (Stanford: Stanford University Press, 2007).

72 Tronti, *Workers and Capital*, 27.
73 Ibid., 242.
74 Ibid., 244.
75 Ibid., 255.
76 Ibid., 255–6.
77 Nanni Balestrini, *We Want Everything*, trans. Rachel Kushner (New York: Verso, 2016), 82.
78 Ibid., 87.
79 E. P. Thompson, *The Making of the English Working Class* (New York: Vintage, 1966), 1.
80 Ibid., 194.
81 Ibid., 713.
82 Rancière, *Proletarian Nights*, ix.
83 Ibid.

5

Baudrillard

Despite his catchphrase—*history is a process without a subject*—Althusser's theory of ideology theorizes that the subject is always-already hailed. The question is: what kind of subjects will be recruited? Everything turns on winning the subject position of the hailing, the position of authority; in other words, everything depends on the struggle to win the subject position of the State. Althusserian ideological theory is itself subject to or subordinated to the logic of the subject, desire, and subjugation. In this respect, it arguably reproduces the very ideology that it critiques. How to break this spiral? This is Baudrillard's question. Baudrillard turns to the object and to a form of theory that I call *objectal* so as to differentiate it from "objectivity."

Precession of the Object

Baudrillard distinguishes between representation and simulation. The two concepts are for Baudrillard opposed. Representation "starts from the principle that the sign and the real are equivalent," writes Baudrillard, "even if this equivalence is utopian, it is a fundamental axiom."[1] "Conversely, simulation," Baudrillard continues, "starts from the *utopia* of this principle of equivalence."[2] Representation as concept is based on a principle of equivalence—utopian at its best—that nonetheless recognizes the discrepancy between sign and real. Simulation by contrast proffers a utopian vision of the unification of sign and real. Disneyland is one of Baudrillard's favorite examples.

Disneyland is not an equivalent representation of something else. It presents itself as a utopia—a no-place—where Disney's imagery and imaginary are realized. "Whereas representation tries to absorb simulation by interpreting it as false representation," writes Baudrillard, "simulation envelops the whole edifice of representation as itself a simulacrum."[3] Representation is premised on the idea of *re-presentation* whereas simulation simulates representation itself and thereby splits representation off from the semblance of reference.

Representation is bound up with the dialectic of reflection as either faithful reflection of reality or perverse ruse that masks reality. Simulation is altogether different for "it bears no relation to any reality whatever: it is its own pure simulacrum."[4]

Ideological critique in its traditional form is bound to the concept of reflection. False consciousness, for example, presupposes that a true consciousness would reflect reality as it truly is. But in simulacral societies reality has become "hyperreal": a condition in which the line between image and the real is obscured. Baudrillard appropriated the term "hyperreal" from the artworld. In the late 1960s and 1970s artists such as Richard Estes refounded representational painting by making paintings based on photographs. Estes's best-known works look like photographs—representations of images—but the worlds they represent are amalgams of multiple photographs. His paintings are simulations of places that do not exist anywhere. And yet this example is at best flawed. Hyperrealist painting "is not theoretically the essence of this [simulacral] form," writes Mike Gane in his invaluable study, "it is but its flawed ironic duplication, since there is still the artist's signature and the 'border that separates' the painted surface of the work of art and the wall of the gallery."[5] Hyperreal societies produce a "kind of fusion of real and imaginary," writes Gane, "so that there is no longer a play of representation based on clearly demarcated separations: the real 'swallows' its alienated double."[6] This cultural shift might be better analogized by the art of Sherrie Levine. In the

1980s, Levine became (in)famous for her photographic reproductions of famous photographs by towering photographers of the first half of the twentieth century such as Walker Evans. Levine's reproductions are not pictures of individuals. They are pictures of pictures or images of representations. Walker photographed subjects; Levine photographed objects. Baudrillard's orientation is affine with Levine's. He is concerned with the simulacrum as object as image-thing. Let us not forget that Baudrillard himself was a serious photographer who well understood (like Levine) that a photograph is an object-image, not a transparent index of the real even if that is still how photography is ideologically metabolized.

The subject is central to any theory of representation since it depends on the dialectic of judgment as to the truth or falsity of any representation. The simulacral condition, however, irradiates the power of the subject. The concept of stable "reality" in simulacral societies cannot be neatly distinguished from the very real shifting paly of images, signs, and codes. This condition demands a break with the subject (knower) to object (representation). It requires a form of thinking that takes the effacement of the line between the imaginary and the real—and with it the classical epistemological subject—as a point of departure. In *Fatal Strategies*, Baudrillard writes that "today the position of the subject has become simply untenable" in comparison to the proliferation of hyperreal objects made of signs, images, and codes.[7] Theory now must, according to Baudrillard, begin anew from the "only possible position ... that of the object."[8] Hyperreality demands a new kind of theory that no longer privileges the subject even in the guise of its deconstruction. "Calling the subject into question," writes Baudrillard, "hasn't changed much concerning the metaphysical postulate of its preeminence."[9] Challenges to the subject have, according to Baudrillard, merely "trapped" the subject "in the melodrama of its own disappearance."[10]

The Object of Post-criticism

The question for Baudrillard is: how to think the object as such? How to grasp it and not bypass it as a mere "detour on the royal road to subjectivity"?[11] Baudrillard argues that to move from the subject to the position of the object requires a break with critique as traditionally practiced. This is already clear in his polemic against Foucault.

Forget Foucault was originally submitted to the influential journal *Critique*. Foucault himself was a member of the journal's editorial board at the time. The article was rejected. The essay, however, is not simply an attack on Foucault. "Foucault" is a cipher for the limits of critique. Baudrillard argues that critique is always entangled and complicit with the power it aims to expose, identify, and critique. Power and critique are locked in a spiral of self-regeneration. Critique vampirically accrues its surplus cultural capital by feeding on power. Baudrillard's post-critical theory—what he calls "theory-fiction"— dispenses with the mimeticism of traditional criticism. It attempts to break the critique-power spiral by refusing the representationalist aesthetic of traditional critique, which redoubles power by re-presenting in critical form.

Post-critical theory is radically anti-mimetic. Much of the controversy that surrounded so-called high theory had to do with the way figures such as Derrida, Deleuze, Guattari, Lyotard, Baudrillard, and others pushed theory toward more literary and more self-referential forms of address. In "experimental" works by Derrida (for example, *Glas*) or Deleuze and Guattari (for example, *A Thousand Plateaus*), as in the later work of Baudrillard (such as *Fatal Strategies*), there is an attempt to push critical writing beyond the confines of critical representationalism.

This fact in no small way is what made theory such a "scandal" as Marc Redfield has shown in his account of the mediatization of theory in the US academy.[12] But in 1983, it was Gregory Ulmer who first noted this shift from representationalist critique toward antimimetic forms of theoretical writing.

In "The Object of Post-criticism" (included in the landmark anthology *The Anti-Aesthetic*), Ulmer argues that the shift away from critical representationalism in then recent theory can be understood as the belated emergence of modernist aesthetics in postmodernist theory. Ulmer writes:

> What is at stake in the controversy surrounding contemporary critical writing is easier to understand when placed in the context of modernism and postmodernism in the arts. The issue is "representation"—specifically, the representation of the object of study in a critical text. Criticism is now being transformed in the same way that literature and the arts were transformed by the avant-garde movements in the early decades of the this [the twentieth] century. The break with "mimesis," with the values and assumptions of "realism," which revolutionized the modernist arts, is now underway (belatedly) in criticism, the chief consequence of which, of course, is a change in the relation of the critical text to its object.[13]

The story of modernist aesthetics, especially in the visual arts, as understood by its major champions such as Clement Greenberg, is the story of artists who turned away from the problem of representation toward an intense concern with the objective materiality of the medium at times to the exclusion of any other concern at all. The Greenbergian theory of modernist painting, for example, holds that the materialist emphasis in modernist painting forced open and maintained a space of relevance for the art of painting in the age of mass media imagery.[14]

But the emphasis on the materiality of art shifted in the 1960s to a broader interest in rethinking painting and sculpture in object-centric terms. This approach to painting and sculpture generated a good deal of polemics in critical writing on the arts in the 1960s between emergent minimalists like Frank Stella, and even more so

Donald Judd, who wanted to flatten the distinction between artworks and objects and post-Greenbergian critics, such as Michael Fried, who were keen to preserve a line of demarcation. The minimalists' interest in challenging the border between objects of art and objects as such, according to Fried, threatened to displace the place for art altogether.[15] What Carter Ratcliff describes as the apodictic aesthetic of minimalist and post-minimalist art—its materialist, declarative, and inexpressive *thereness*—is indexed in Judd's rejection of the term *sculpture* for that of "specific objects."[16]

Modernists like Fried, and minimalists like Judd, represented a tension in the art of the 1960s that was galvanized and driven by a critical interest in the relation between art and objecthood. It was as if an entire dialectic had been squeezed into that precarious dash between the two words of the term "art-object." We might then say (to revise Ulmer slightly) that post-criticism represents less a modernist aesthetics in theoretical and critical writing than a postmodernist preoccupation with the object. Baudrillard's writing affirms an anti-Friedian *objectal* aesthetics. He is not alone. Derrida also exemplifies this tendency in *Glas* of 1974.

Glas is made of two juxtaposed columns. The left-side column is a commentary on Hegel and the right is a commentary on Jean Genet. The theme of the text is the question of the family seen from these two sides: philosophy and literature, the nineteenth and twentieth centuries, Germany and France, heterosexual and queer, and much more. It is a dialectic (Hegel) and a dialogue (Genet) that calls into question the differences between genres while not effacing the distinction in the name of an ideality of "pure" writing. The boundaries of genres are made visible by their intersectional and conflictual cohabitation on the same page.

The very physicality of *Glas*—its objectality—is striking. It is about the dimensions of a phonograph sleeve. The binding, layout, and the text's typographical idiosyncrasies make the book difficult reading. It is not simply difficult to interpret but actually difficult to physically read. The physical difficulty of *Glas* won't let the reader forget the fact they are holding a thing, an object. *Glas* binds the relation between philosophy and literature to the question of the objectal conditions of the book. I agree fully with Geoffrey Hartman's advice to look at "*Glas* as a work of art."[17] With *Glas* Derrida, notes Hartman, joined the ranks of "so many contemporary artists ... [at the time by] materializing [the] imprint of words."[18] Derrida's *Glas* can be fruitfully compared with the works of a number of conceptual artists of the 1970s, such as Joseph Kosuth. Much conceptual art of the period, as with *Glas*, strategically materializes and spatializes language and thereby mitigates the effectivity of language's referential function by overdetermining its objectality. Contra Lucy Lippard's well-known claim that conceptual art of the 1970s amounted to the "dematerialization of the art-object," conceptual art and high theory of the time show the materiality of writing.[19] Whatever reference is blocked from view is blocked by the apodictic *thereness* and *isness* of the materiality of the texts themselves. We are made to *see writing*.

This turn in critical-theoretical writing away from referentiality to objectality is particularly acute in Baudrillard's later work. Whereas *The System of Objects* lays out meta-theoretical conditions for a possible taxonomy or system of objects; Baudrillard's later work (post-1975) gives up the ghost of this dream of a complete theory of objects for a more experimental, literary, non-referential mode of writing in which the text itself achieves a kind of objectal status. We might literalize Ulmer's wager and say: Baudrillard's late work evinces a turn to *the object* of (or as) post-criticism. Baudrillard's later theoretical writing challenges phenomena and objects by means of the phenomenal and objectal powers of writing. This is indexed, if somewhat enigmatically articulated, in Baudrillard's *The Ecstasy of Communication* of 1987. Allow me to quote from it at length.

To be a reflection of the real, or to enter into a relation of critical negativity with the real, cannot be theory's goal. This was the pious vow of ... [the] Enlightenment, and to this day it determines ... intellectual moral standing. But today this appealing dialectic seems unsettled. What good is theory? If the world is hardly compatible with the concept of the real which we impose upon it, the function of theory is certainly not to reconcile, but on the contrary, to seduce, to wrest things from their condition, to force them into an over-existence which is incompatible with the real. Theory pays dearly for this in a prophetic autodestruction. ... It ... must deploy the same strategy as its object. If it [theory] no longer aspires to a discourse of truth, theory must assume the form of a world from which truth has withdrawn. And thus it becomes its very object.[20]

Theory should no longer orient itself according to the epistemological assumptions of ideological critique *qua* the project of unmasking societal illusions to reveal the real. In a world of simulacra—a world in which simulations do not refer but produce (and therefore precede) reference—truth can no longer be defended according to the metric set by the appearance-reality axis. In a world where the appearance-reality dialectic "seems unsettled," theory can still play a role. But it can no longer be the cry of the *subject of truth* against illusion but should, argues Baudrillard, be a strategic "seduction" carried out on the objectal plane.

In some ways this idea of the object as model for theory remained only an ideal for Baudrillard. Even in his later work, he still does (partially) engage in mimetic commentary and critique. His late style still telegraphically signals a certain fidelity to critical practice of old. But its objectality does mark a break and a decisive one in Baudrillard's theoretical production.

Baudrillard's American publishers—Semiotext(e) especially and to a lesser extent Verso—perhaps unwittingly amplified this dimension by publishing a series of his texts in square formats that make the experience of reading them objectal in ways that are comparable to the experience of reading Derrida's *Glas*. The objectal theme of Baudrillard's later works is underscored, for example, in the 1996 Verso edition of *The System of Objects*. The cover image is James Rosenquist's 1961 pop art painting: *I love you with my Ford*. The painting juxtaposes three stacked registers of imagery: the hood of a Ford, the figure of a woman kissing (and blending with) the hood of the car, and finally, a field of Franco-American spaghetti. The painting suggests a world in which the object indeed seduces, in which visceral feeling is prepackaged like canned spaghetti which, in the painting, resembles human guts. Rosenquist suggests that we become subjects of desire (and otherwise) by becoming objectal. This is simply to say, with Marx, that under capital subjects are produced by the siren call of commodity fetishism. Social relations between people function as relations among things: *I love you with my Ford*.

Post-subject-centric theory has birthed a series of dissolutions, deconstructions, and demystifications. But all this, for Baudrillard, is "the melodrama" of the subject's disappearance. By "object," notes Baudrillard, we "should understand ... not the 'alienated' object in the process of de-alienation, the enslaved object claiming its autonomy as a subject, but the object such as it challenges the subject, and pushes back upon its own impossible position."[21] The object as such, for Baudrillard, should not be considered according to any logic of the subject.

The object belongs to another order of logic entirely. Nor should one think that the object is simply an instance of radical alterity for that otherness *only exists for the subject*. The object, notes Baudrillard, "knows no alterity and is inalienable. It is not divided with itself—which is the destiny of the subject."[22] But there is alas no way to *think* objectality without reinscribing it within the logic of the subject. The object as such "is what has disappeared on the horizon of the subject," writes Baudrillard, "and it is from the depths of this disappearance that it envelops the subject in its fatal strategy. It is the subject then that disappears from the horizon of the object."[23] This is both the promise and paradox of Baudrillard's post-critical writings.

Curvature

Baudrillard's post-critical texts are marked by a new language cloned from physics and cosmology. In this he follows a cultural trend. Where once questions concerning the nature of reality, god, and so forth were the source of conceptual wonder, today it is the matter of matter, particles, black holes, and so on. The fact, for example, that books by the likes of Stephen Hawking and Brian Greene are bestsellers has to do with the way that scientific culture has absorbed the outer zones of wonder once occupied by metaphysics. I want to parse Baudrillard's "scientific" rhetoric and focus on his language of curvature and spheres. Let me simply enumerate a number of invocations of curved spaces.

1. "[T]he malicious curvature [of the hyperreal] … puts an end to the horizon of 'meaning.'"[24]
2. "[T]he [social] masses function as a gigantic black hole which inexorably inflects, bends and distorts all energy and light radiation approaching it; an implosive sphere in which the curvature of space accelerates, in which all dimensions curve back on themselves and 'involve' to the point of annihilation."[25]
3. "The hyperreal is the abolition of the real not by violent destruction, but by assumption, elevation to the strength of the model … the model acts as a sphere of absorption of the real."[26]
4. "the sphere of the virtual"[27]

5. "This is the ideal form of simulation: collapse of poles, orbital circulation of models (this is also the matrix of every implosive process)."[28]
6. "like two ends of a curved mirror ... [a] vicious curvature ... All the referentials intermingle their discourses in a circular, Moebian compulsion"[29]
7. "In this passage to a space whose curvature is no longer that of the real, nor of truth, the age of simulation begins."[30]

The language of curvature, orbits, implosive trajectories, black holes, and so on don't merely function as metaphors in Baudrillard's theoretical writing. Metaphor belongs to the orders of the real and the referential. The simulacrum does not refer to reality: it realizes it. Reference implies distance, the dialectic of figure and ground, and indexical grammar. The hyperreal implodes distance, curving the index back on itself, obliterating the distance between metaphor and metaphorized. Frank Stella famously said of his black line paintings of the 1960s: "these paths lead only into painting."[31] As for Baudrillard, *his lines of theory lead only into hyperreal theory*. The "malicious curvature" of Baudrillard's work is self-implosive. It is not simply that it swallows the real; it swallows the very idea of reference itself. His theoretical prose condenses to a singularity of "divine irreference."[32] After 1975, Baudrillard's theoretical production becomes its own object. Its stylistic and textual density turns its theoretical force upon itself. Theory now becomes a black hole. Theory now, Baudrillard notes, "becomes its very object."[33] *The theory of the simulacrum is hyperrealized as the simulacrum of theory.* Hyperreal theory, like the Moebius strip, turns back on itself. This twisted involuted spiral lends Baudrillard's writing what he describes as a kind of vertiginous "giddiness."[34]

There is certainly an aesthetic of giddiness in Baudrillard's late theory. Is he saying that the real has disappeared? If so, then he is referring to a historical event and his theory is referential. Or is he only performing in the space of theoretical writing the disappearance of reference? Is the latter a symptom of the disappearance of the real from thought? Such questions perhaps wrongly assume that Baudrillard knows. It presupposes another god-like reference: authorial intent. Baudrillard notes:

> I admit, that the question of theory troubles me. Where is theory situated today? Is it completely satellized? Is it wandering in realms which no longer have anything to do with real facts? What is analysis? As long as you consider that there is a real world, then by the same token there is a possible position for theory. Let us say a dialectical position, for the sake of argument. Theory and reality can still be exchanged at some point—and that is ideality. ... That is not my position anymore. Moreover, it never was. But I have never succeeded in formulating it. In my opinion, theory is simply a challenge to the real.[35]

There is little to go on here. But to try and decipher Baudrillard's theory by means of discerning his intent is to miss the point. The point of his later work is to lend theory shape—to extend it from the point of the subject—into a "malicious curvature" that circles back on itself, enclosing theory in its own objectality. In its ideal objectal form theory becomes a "fatal" theory or "strategy." Fatal strategy has a two-fold meaning. It refers to the death of theory in the traditional, referential, and critical sense. And it means turning this "fate" into a matter of strategy. If the real is fated to disappear then theory must disappear into this very disappearance. It must tie its fate to the hyperreal by becoming something more than critical. It must become objectal and having achieved this object state it is also dead on arrival. "Therefore theory, and this is a paradoxical proposition," notes Baudrillard, "becomes fatal. It makes itself object."[36] Theory can relinquish the dialectics of critique and reality, but at the price of its death—at the price of its *becoming-object*.

The Specter of the Real

Baudrillard's best-known thesis is also his most provocative: *the death of the real.* This axiom has provoked the ire of critics who cite it often as evidence of the supposed shallowness and easy-going relativism of "postmodernism." Baudrillard himself never liked the term. "One should ask whether postmodernism, the postmodern, has a meaning. It doesn't as far as I am concerned," notes Baudrillard.[37] The word is "an expression, a word which people use but which explains nothing. It's not even a concept."[38] Baudrillard's comment here is indicative of a certain critical persistence even in his late work.

Baudrillard's later work does not abandon meaning to the endless play of the sign and the simulacrum. Rather, he tries to reimagine what theory still can do in a world that is dominated by the simulacrum. Indeed, the very idea of the death of the real grants it a kind of funerary grandeur that seems quite out of place if Baudrillard is simply ready to have done with the matter of the real. Recall that in *Simulations*, Baudrillard inverts Borges's story of the mapmakers and the empire. Allow me to quote Baudrillard at length:

> If we were able to take the finest allegory of simulation the Borges tale where the cartographers of the Empire draw up a map so detailed that it ends up exactly covering the territory (but where the decline of the Empire sees this map become frayed and finally ruined, a few shreds still discernible in the deserts—the metaphysical beauty of this ruined abstraction, bearing witness to an Imperial pride and rotting like a carcass, returning as an aging double ends up being confused with the real thing)—then this fable has come full circle for us, and has nothing but the discrete charm of second-order simulacra. Abstraction, today is no longer that of the map, the double, the mirror or the concept. Simulation is no longer that of a territory, a referential being or a substance. It is the generation of models of a real without origin or reality: a

> hyperreal. ... [I]f we were to revive the fable today, it would be the territory whose shreds are slowly rotting across the map. It is the real, and not the map, whose vestiges subsist here and there, in the deserts which are no longer those of the Empire, but our own. The desert of the real itself.[39]

Simulacral societies produce reality effects by models without origin. But "vestiges" of the real still "subsist here and there." Baudrillard never contests the matter-of-fact reality that things happen and things exist, including death and disaster. But "the real" or "reality" are not simply other names for that which exists. For Baudrillard, "the real" and "reality" are *concepts*. These terms do not refer to what exists but to *systems* for drawing up lines of demarcation and distinctions to conceptually parse what exists.

The concepts of "the real" and "reality" are part of the inheritance of Western metaphysics. Appearance/truth, signifier/signified, subjective/objective, model/reference, and so on belong to a pre-simulacral conceptual universe. But in simulacral societies, the distinction between models that refer and models without origin has withered. The conceptual universe of the real can still be (and still is) applied even by Baudrillard himself. The very fact that he *conceptualizes and historicizes the simulacrum indicates that*. There are instances when, for example, the pseudo-reference of the hyperreal is revealed or instances that make palpable the weight of reality. But these are scattered across the simulacral field. It is as if the continent of the real has eroded into an archipelago.

Baudrillard's thesis should therefore be interpreted with some nuance. If the real still subsists in scattered and withered vestiges, then this thesis is better read not as a statement referring to what has happened but to what *is happening and must happen* given the drift of simulacral society. To say the real is dead is like saying of the dying man: *he's a dead man*. The fatality of the real should, I think, be read in the double sense that Baudrillard gives to his concept, "fatal strategies": destiny and finality. There is here a vestige of critical theory in precisely the diagnostic and prognostic sense of critical theory proper to pre-simulacral times. Baudrillard still plays the role of the demythologizing critic in attempting to construct a conceptual system to theorize and historicize the simulacrum from the vantage point of those remaining vestiges of the real. All this is of the greatest consequence for constructing a possible Baudrillardian theory of ideology. But to do so we must make another "detour" as Althusser liked to say. We must detour through the spirit of Derrida.

Spirit and Specter

In 1993, Derrida turned to Marx at the very moment when the end of history was being announced. The death of "actually existing socialism" left the specters of Marx (and Marxism) free to haunt the political and theoretical imaginary as once communism had in the pages of Marx and Engels's *Manifesto*. The very moment when the death of the Soviet Union was manifestly evident, Derrida chose to awaken the spirit of Marx in his *Specters of Marx*. The Right's triumphalist glee at 1989 belied a deep anxiety that the death of State socialism in the East did not guarantee the death of Marx (or Marxism). The death of actually existing socialism reawakened the specter of communism's ghost. Ventriloquizing neoliberal anxiety, Derrida writes:

> A still worried sign of relief: let us make sure that in the future it does not come back; in the future said the powers of old Europe in the last century [the nineteenth], it must not incarnate itself, either publicly or in secret. In the future, we hear everywhere today, it must not re-incarnate itself; it must not be allowed to come back since it is past.[40]

The specter of communism invoked by Marx and Engels in *The Communist Manifesto* was a spectral threat to the capitalist powers of "old Europe" at the end of the nineteenth century. It was a threat of a possible future to come. At the beginning of the end of the twentieth century, following the death of the Soviet Union, the specter reappears. Communism and capitalism are materialisms haunted by specters. Money, property, commodities, value itself are indices, traces, spectral vestiges of the spirit of capital. Marx and his adversaries thus share this modern antipathy to ghosts. Derrida writes:

> This hostility toward ghosts, a terrified hostility that sometimes fends off terror with a burst of laughter, is perhaps what Marx will have had in common with his adversaries. He too will have tried to *conjure* (away) the ghosts, and everything that was neither life nor death, namely, the re-apparition of an apparition that will never be either the appearing or the disappeared, the phenomenon or its contrary. He will have tried to conjure (away) the ghosts *like* the conspirators of old Europe on whom the *Manifesto* declares war.[41]

Derrida draws a conceptual distinction between "specter" and "spirit." Specter is a material "thing," whereas spirit always transcends the order of things.[42] The specter "assumes a body, it incarnates itself."[43] The spirit takes form as specter, visage, body, voice, shadowy figure, and so on. The spirit haunts in the *form* of the specter. Derrida writes:

> [T]he specter is a paradoxical incorporation, the becoming-body, a certain phenomenal and carnal form of the spirit. It becomes, rather, some "thing" that remains difficult to name: neither soul nor body, and both one and the other. For it is flesh and phenomenality that give to the spirit its spectral apparition, but which disappear right away in the apparition, in the very coming of the *revenant* or the return of the specter.[44]

Derrida's distinction enables the conceptualization of the relation between the idea (or ideal) of Marxism, communism, or capitalism and its incarnate forms or spectral traces. On the one hand, it is possible to conceptualize the spirit (of Marxism, Communism, and capitalism) but only negatively as that which is always-already mediated by the spectral forms that determine its very thinkability. Let us now apply this analytic to Baudrillard's objectal theory.

Spectrality and Objectality

The objectal form of Baudrillard's writing I suggest is a spectral instance of critique in post-critical form. Baudrillard's post-critical, anti-mimetic, objectal mode of theory is haunted by the spirit of the criticism of old. This is in no way a condemnation. Rather, it is to my thinking what is most interesting about it. The object for Baudrillard is an orientation, a horizon, a potential.

But his writing never achieves pure objectal form. The spirit of the *subject of critique* remains a haunting specter in Baudrillard's later work. The objectal and post-critical form telegraphically relays the spirit of ideological critique in a spectral form that removes all but the barest traces of subject-centric thinking from its horizon. The result is a haunted conception of the object. "There are some problematics which are quite insoluble today in terms of psychology or sociology," notes Baudrillard, "a whole area of contention, growing all the time, and which will never be recycled. That is why we must try to jump over the wall, cross to the side of the object, side with it against the subject."[45] The phrasing is telling: "we must try" to "cross to the side of the object." Baudrillard's post-critical phase is this very jump, this attempt, to "cross to the side of the object." But what happens to this "we" who makes it over the wall? In the spirit of Derrida, I want to suggest that this subject, "we," remains a haunting presence that enables the *object of theory* to go "against the subject."

The spirit of critique animates the specter of the *object* of Baudrillard's post-critical writings. Put plainly, the "strategy" of Baudrillard's "fatal" or "objectal" theory is that the subject of critique haunts the position of the object. His post-critical work adopts the language of strategic discourse. He divides this discourse into "fatal" and "banal" strategies. Fatal strategy is theory in the objectal mode; banal strategy is critique in the old subject-centric mode. The latter is banalized by the hyperproliferation of the object world and its increasing sovereignty over that of the subject. As Baudrillard explains:

> Theory for me is a fatal strategy—perhaps the only one. That's the whole difference between a banal theory and a fatal theory: in the first the subject believes himself to be cleverer than the object; in the second the object is always supposed to be cleverer, more cynical and more inspired than the subject, whom he awaits ironically at the end of the detour.[46]

The language of strategy that marks Baudrillard's post-critical work signals his abandonment of anything like a neutral theoretical ideal. The point is to go "against the subject" by showing its pride to be fallacious in the face of the increasing power of the world of the object. The object world is what compels "us" as spectral subjects.

Reading Althusser Fatally

Althusser's attempt to constitute a "general theory" of ideology rooted in a materialist epistemology enables us to consider how material practices and institutions produce the subject. This theory establishes a perspective rid of the whole problem of ideology as a matter of consciousness, which is to say the whole Hegelian legacy of the "subject of consciousness," "false consciousness," and so on. Althusser's theory attempts to show that this "idealist" conception of ideology is itself ideological because it rests on a fundamentally anti-materialist basis, which presumes that thought (understood as immaterial or "spiritual") is the origin of material reality. On Althusser's reading, this very idealist conception of ideology is in fact materially produced by institutions, deployments of power, and coercive State and civil practices. But seen through Baudrillard's frame something else emerges.

Althusser begins with the materiality of the apparatuses (objects) of State and ideological repression. It is on this basis that he establishes the theoretical genesis of the ideology of the subject. Theoretical priority is given to the object in the form of the apparatuses of ideological and State control, which constitute the subject through interpellation. But is there not at the metatheoretical level a reprioritization of the subject? Does not the text reconstruct the figure of the master-pedagogue (à la Rancière) who once again arrives to teach us a lesson? Yes and no.

Althusser first conceived Marxist theory as an *autonomous science*. In *Reading Capital*, Althusser argues that theory is a truthful way of seeing or "sighting" things, but this seeing is not that of a subject of consciousness. He writes:

> Any object or problem situated on the terrain and within the horizon, i.e., in the definite structured field of the theoretical problematic of a given theoretical discipline, is visible. We must take these words literally. The sighting is thus no longer the act of an individual subject, endowed with the faculty of "vision" which he exercises either attentively or distractedly; the sighting is the act of its structural conditions, it is the relation of immanent reflection between the field of the problematic and *its* objects and *its* problems.[47]

Theory here is analogized as "structured field" or a "terrain" of visibility. Phenomena are made visible by the immanent "structural conditions" of the field of theory itself. The visibility of truth, phenomena, and so on are made visible in (and as) theory. The theoretical field is an object immanently governed by its own theoretico-logical structures and not by the theorist or any other individual subject. Theoretical "sighting" is a function of the immanent theoretico-logical relations established between a "theoretical field of the problematic and *its* objects and *its* problems." The italicized "its" emphasizes this non-subject-oriented conception of theory or *theory of theory*. If theoretical sighting is conditioned by the immanent relation between the field of a given theoretical problematic and *its* object, then finally Althusser's theory of theory can be revised in Baudrillardian terms as an intra-objectal theory of theory.

Althusser theorizes theoretical insight as a function of the immanent relation between two objects—the theoretical field of a given problematic and *its* objects—and not that between a subject of knowledge and the object of that knowledge. Ideology too in the same text is treated as an a-subjective force. Althusser argues that ideology can become visible precisely within the field of a given theoretical problematic as *Marx's theory* (not Marx the man) showed in pointing out the errors of classical political economy. Althusser writes:

> Every imaginary (ideological) posing of a problem (which may be imaginary, too) in fact carries it in a determinate problematic, which defines both the possibility and the form of the posing of this problem. This problematic *recurs* as its mirror-image in the solution given to this problem by virtue of the mirror action peculiar to the ideological imagination.[48]

Ideology can parasitically embed itself within a given theoretical problematic and, symptomatically, this ideological element *recurs* or repeats (as in a mirror) in the theoretical operation itself. If the theoretical field has been ideologically (rather than critically) constructed then it will reproduce that very ideology in the posing and solving of questions within its visible purview. But here the a-subjective (or objectal) conception of the field of theory runs into serious problems. Who or what constructs the frame or field of theory? Can it be said to construct itself? Does theory have its own agency? Matters are more complicated when we turn to the essay on ideology. By the time he wrote that, Althusser had firmly rejected the "theoreticist" approach of *Reading Capital* and his other writings of that period. He rejects the idea of theory as an abstract and autonomous science.

The publication of *Lenin and Philosophy* marks a determined effort to theorize theory as embedded in the class struggle against the philosophical forces of idealism and the political forces of capital. Theory, understood as immanent to class struggle, would seem to require a return of the subject in the form of the partisan who wields theory as a weapon. Althusser suggests as much when he writes that "philosophy is a certain continuation of politics ... philosophy represents scientificity in politics, with the classes engaged in class struggle."[49] Philosophy or theory represents the interest of scientific rigor in politics. But this is not a disinterested concern for scientificity. It is a partisan struggle allied with the class struggle in an effort to win over the very idea of science for the proletariat. The move from a "theoreticist" conception of theory to that of theory as an activity of the politically committed partisan was, for Althusser, a move from a philosopher of Marxism to a *communist in philosophy*. As he notes in an interview with Maria Antonietta Macciochi, "[t]o become a Communist in philosophy is to become a partisan and artisan of Marxist-Leninist philosophy: of dialectical materialism."[50] The combination of words here, "partisan and artisan," is of crucial importance.

To be a Communist in philosophy demands a new practice of philosophy (inaugurated by Lenin according to Althusser), according to which one treats philosophy as part of the class struggle. Philosophy is "nothing but a tendency struggle."⁵¹ Even more directly, Althusser states in *How to Be a Marxist in Philosophy*:

> For, since every philosophy is in a state of war, at the limit, with the other philosophical tendency, materialist or idealist, it must necessarily take preventative action against the enemy in order to get the better of him; in other words, it must preventatively occupy its adversary's positions, even if that means cloaking itself in its adversary's arguments.⁵²

The cause of philosophy after Lenin (or in his name) is to do battle against the allied forces of idealism and capitalism. But to take and win ground requires at times "cloaking" philosophical theses in the "adversary's arguments." Might there be something of this strategy at work intentionally or not in the ISAs essay?

The essay seeks to secure a materialist theory of ideology and thus to beat back the forces of revisionism. The essay is an intra-Marxist war against revisionism. It takes aim at the citadel of the humanist subject and the idealist conceit of consciousness. But the dramaturgical quality of the essay with its *pivotal* scene articulates a drama of the individual *cum* subject. Judith Butler notably detected this unresolved humanist concession to the primacy of the individual who then becomes a subject. But what accounts for the production of the individual? Whence did it come?⁵³ The use of metaphor, analogy, dramatic presentation, all of which Althusser insistently asks us to overlook, is perhaps the cloaking device that enables him to frame and situate an argument against the subject in a form whose intelligibility is framed and determined by the aesthetic resources of humanist theater. The message might be that if the ideology of the subject is "eternal" or at least always-already at work, then the question is not how to escape ideology but how to do battle on the field of ideology itself. As Banu Bargu argues:

> Althusser's theoretical solution to the aporia of interpellation ... seems less about working out how a subjectivity could be free

from the subjection in interpellation than about the espousal of the active struggle over the direction of the effects of subjection, having conceded the constancy of subjection. Politics must work with and within dominant ideology, rendering popular opinion or the masses' achievement of mastery over their own subjectivation the real theater of struggle.[54]

The role of theatrical thinking is crucial in Althusser's work. In *For Marx* Althusser devotes theoretical reflection on the materialist theater of Carlo Bertolazzi and its role in ideological battle. In the ISAs essay, he sets his own theory within a dramaturgical frame in order to secure a materialist theory of ideology by weaponizing the aesthetic resources of humanist theater.

Althusser's theory treats ideology as an object, an apparatus, that constructs and compels the subject. It is objectal in its orientation. But its allegorical drama pivots on the pivoting individual of humanism itself. This is comparable to Baudrillard's objectal theory in that it presents less a pure object than a *haunted object* animated in this case by the artifice of the drama of the humanist subject precisely so as to subject it to critique. The artifice, the constructedness, the objectality of state, and civil apparatuses are represented precisely as an object of critique and this is reaffirmed and ramified by presenting it within the artifice and constructedness of Althusser's theoretical theater. There is a haunting of the objects of theory here, ideological and repressive apparatuses, and the entire theory itself, as theater, is haunted by the specter of the ideology of the author or the theater director who stages the appearance of the object of ideology, namely the object *qua* subject of ideology.

Are we not still trapped in a spiral? How can theory move beyond the dogmatics of subject and object? How can it move beyond the problem of the prioritization of one over the other? How does one do theory non-ideologically? It is to Laruelle's nonstandard philosophy that we finally turn to sketch a possible solution.

Notes

1. Jean Baudrillard, *Simulations*, trans. Paul Foss, Paul Patton and Philip Beitchman (Los Angeles: Semiotext(e), 1983), 11.
2. Ibid.
3. Ibid.
4. Ibid.
5. Mike Gane, *Jean Baudrillard: In Radical Uncertainty* (London: Pluto Press, 2000), 41.
6. Ibid.
7. Jean Baudrillard, *Fatal Strategies*, trans. Philippe Beitchman and W. G. J. Niesluchowski (Los Angeles: Semiotext(e), 2008), 143.
8. Ibid.
9. Ibid., 142.
10. Ibid.
11. Ibid., 141.
12. See Marc Redfield, *Theory at Yale: The Strange Case of Deconstruction in America* (Brooklyn: Fordham University Press, 2015).
13. Gregory Ulmer, "The Object of Post-Criticism," in *The Anti-Aesthetic: Essays on Postmodern Culture*, ed. Hal Foster (Port Townsend: Bay Press, 1983), 83.
14. See Clement Greenberg, "Modernist Painting," in *Modern Art and Modernism: A Critical Anthology*, ed. Francis Frascina and Charles Harrison (New York: Routledge, 2019).
15. See Michael Fried, *Art and Objecthood: Essays and Reviews* (Chicago: The University of Chicago Press, 1998).
16. See Donald Judd, "Specific Objects," in *Art in Theory, 1900–200: An Anthology of Changing Ideas*, ed. Charles Harrison and Paul Wood (Malden: Blackwell Publishing, 2003).
17. Geoffrey Hartman, *Saving the Text: Literature, Derrida, Philosophy* (Baltimore: The Johns Hopkins University Press, 1981), 90.
18. Ibid.
19. Lucy R. Lippard, *Six Years: The Dematerialization of the Art Object from 1966–1972* (Berkeley: University of California Press, 2001).

20 Jean Baudrillard, "Why Theory?," in *Hatred of Capitalism*, ed. Chris Krauss and Sylvère Lotringer (Los Angeles: Semiotext(e), 2001), 129.
21 Ibid., 143–4.
22 Ibid., 144.
23 Ibid.
24 Ibid., 45.
25 Jean Baudrillard, *In the Shadow of the Silent Majorities, or the End of the Social, and Other Essays*, trans. Paul Foss, John Johnston and Paul Patton (New York: Semiotext(e), 1983), 9.
26 Ibid., 84.
27 Jean Baudrillard, *The Intelligence of Evil or the Lucidity Pact*, trans. Chris Turner (London: Bloomsbury Academic, 2013), 58.
28 Baudrillard, *In the Shadow of the Silent Majorities*, 21.
29 Baudrillard, *Simulations*, 35.
30 Ibid., 3–4.
31 https://www.moma.org/collection/works/80316.
32 Baudrillard, *Simulations*, 5.
33 Baudrillard, "Why Theory?,"129.
34 Jean Baudrillard, *Forget Foucault* (New York: Semiotext(e), 1983), 81.
35 Ibid., 124.
36 Mike Gane, ed. *Baudrillard Live: Selected Interviews* (London: Routledge, 1993), 56.
37 Ibid., 21.
38 Ibid.
39 Baudrillard, *Simulations*, 1–2.
40 Jacques Derrida, *Specters of Marx: The State of Debt, the Work of Mourning, and the New International*, trans. Peggy Kamuf (New York: Routledge, 1994), 48.
41 Ibid., 58.
42 Ibid., 4.
43 Ibid.
44 Ibid., 5.
45 Gane, *Baudrillard Live*, 39.
46 Ibid.

47 Althusser, *Reading Capital*, 24.
48 Ibid., 264–5.
49 Louis Althusser, *Lenin and Philosophy and Other Essays*, 40.
50 Ibid., 2.
51 Ibid., 34.
52 Louis Althusser, *How to Be a Marxist in Philosophy*, trans. G. M. Goshgarian (London: Bloomsbury Academic, 2017), 59.
53 See Judith Butler, *The Psychic Life of Power: Theories in Subjection* (Stanford: Stanford University Press, 1997).
54 Banu Bargu, "Althusser's Materialist Theater: Ideology and Its Aporias," *Differences: A Journal of Feminist and Cultural Studies* 26, no. 3 (2015): 81–106, 89.

6

Laruelle

Non-philosophy

To begin it will be useful to situate Laruelle's concept of "photographism." The term appears in a set of essays dedicated to the concept of "non-photography." Laruelle's *The Concept of Non-photography* is a dense set of essays. The title is telling. It refers to the fact that his concern is not actual photographs or photographic practices. Rather, his interest is to identify and develop a theory of imageless photographic thinking immanent to the practice of standard philosophy. "Non-photography" is a microcosm of his larger project of "non-philosophy" or as he has more recently called it "non-standard philosophy." It is, to use another term that appears frequently in *The Concept of Non-photography*, an edge in the larger "fractal" of non-standard philosophy. There is a profound symmetry in all of Laruelle's recent projects. One can enter non-philosophy from almost any point—from his writings on photography to that of identity—and one will find that the basic axiomatics of the project repeats at each level or in each dimension of the project.

So, what is non-philosophy? This implies that we know what "standard philosophy" is. Laruelle's answer to put it simply in a phrase is: *standard philosophy is decision on the real*. Philosophy decides the real (of reality, ethics, politics, etc.) because it presupposes it has sufficient conceptual resources to decide these matters. This presupposition Laruelle terms principle of sufficient philosophy (PSP). Non-philosophy inverts this presupposition. It axiomatically presumes that philosophy is *insufficient* to decide the real. This has as much to do with directionality as it does with epistemology. The real has a "unilateral" relation to thought. The real "acts" in one direction. Whatever philosophy decides about the real is itself an instance *in* the real of which philosophical operativity is one of its "effects." Terms like "acts" and "effects" have to be put in scare quotes here because the real is prior to (and inclusive of) the concepts of causation that philosophy imposes on it. Philosophy (and all thought) is always-already part of the real and determined by it but, Laruelle insists, only in *the last instance*.

Althusser follows Engels in asserting the determinative power of the economy only in the last instance; Laruelle radicalizes the concept of the last instance and applies it to the question of the real. For both, this "in the last instance" is an instance that "never comes."[1] For Althusser the instance of the pure determinative power of the economic never purely shows itself as it is always bound up with other instances in an overdetermined conjuncture of forces: the base is *theoretically* isolatable from the superstructure, but the two never operate in isolation from one another. Likewise, for Laruelle, philosophy never operates in isolation from the structurally determinative effects of the real. Yet this determination by the real is never an instance *for philosophy alone* since philosophy can never isolate itself from the real of which it is part. The real that philosophy claims to capture by means of decision blinds it to its determination by the real in the last instance. These then are the basic axioms of non-philosophy.

Photographism

The concept of "photographism" designates a trait that Laruelle detects in the long iterative history of light as metaphor in philosophy from the sun of the Idea in Plato to the light of Reason in the Enlightenment.

"No point in trying to separate philosophy from ... [the] photographic legend that encircles it," writes Laruelle, "philosophy is nothing other than that legend of the fulgurant illumination of things ... that founds the photographocentric destiny of the West."[2] Laruelle argues that a repeated motif of philosophy is the dream of the illumination and capture of the real.

The emergence of photographic technologies for Laruelle is but the mechanical realization of this philosophical dream. It must be emphasized that this was (and can only be) a *dream*. Photography can capture visual instances. But it never does so empirically. It can only do so *photographically*. As Vilém Flusser points out, photography is a *theoretical apparatus*.

Analog and digital photographic technologies do not simply capture their subjects—they *interpret them*. Black-and-white photography, for example, mechanically transcodes the spectrum of visible light into gray scale. Flusser writes:

> There cannot be black-and-white states of things in the world because black-and-white are borderline, "ideal cases:" black is the total absence of all oscillations contained in light, white the total presence of all the elements of oscillation. "Black" and "white" are concepts, e.g. theoretical concepts of optics. As black-and-white states of things are theoretical, they can never actually exist in the world. But black-and-white photographs do actually exist because they are images of concepts belonging to the theory of optics, i.e. they arise out of this theory.[3]

A digital or analog camera is designed or programmed to capture visual phenomena in particular ways. The camera's program corresponds to a specific theory of optics. The program is a model of what looking should be for the camera in terms of focus, color, etc. Photographic images are in that sense images of an underlying theory of seeing not a theory-free capture of what is there.

Laruelle agrees with Flusser that photographic technologies and practices are underwritten by certain theoretical or philosophical commitments concerning optics and visuality broadly. Second, that because of that anything like a "philosophy of photography"—and here he diverges from Flusser—leads into an infinite metatheoretical regress. Philosophy of photography could only be philosophy of philosophy, a conceptualization of concepts, a theoretical apparatus of capture constructed to capture a theoretical apparatus of capture. A philosophy of photography on this score is always-already metaphilosophy.

Philosophy and photography are underwritten by the "technological" determinants of their respective theoretical apparatuses of capture. For, as Laruelle notes, long "before the invention of corresponding technology, a veritable automatism of photographic repetition traverses western thought."[4] The photographocentric thought that philosophy is the writing (graphy) of the light (photo) of reason is precisely what Laruelle seeks to displace. By the same token, he wants to "disencumber the theory of photography" from philosophy. He wants to free photography from its subordination to any philosophy of photography, which is always-already a photographocentric discourse on photography. His aim is to think the "essence" of photography by subtracting photography from philosophy. The stakes of the problem are clearly spelled out. "If we wish simply to describe or think the essence of photography," writes Laruelle, "it is from this hybrid of philosophy as transcendental photography that we must deliver ourselves."[5] The problem is to "think the photographical outside every vicious circle, on the basis of thinking," writes Laruelle, "and perhaps of a 'shot' ... absolutely and right from the start divested of the spirit of photography."[6] The problem then is to *take a shot* at thinking photography by divesting it of its philosophical spirit or its otherwise speculative capture by the terms and hierarchies of philosophy such as image/referent, subject/object, truth/falsity, real/simulation, and so on.

To think photography non-philosophically also means refusing all art-historical and media-theoretic frameworks for these are essentially philosophies of art and media. Laruelle writes:

> Here is the first meaning of "non-photography": this word does not designate some new technique, but a new description and conception of the essence of photography and of the practice that arises within it; of its relation to philosophy; of the necessity no longer to think it through philosophy and its diverse "positions," but to seek an absolutely non-onto-photo-logical thinking of essence, so as to think it correctly, without aporias, circles or infinite metaphors, what photography is and what it can do.[7]

Non-photography names a "description and conception of the essence" of photography and photographic practices. But this "essence" is not essence as understood philosophically. It cannot mean an ontological definition or conception. It would be an essence of photography as such determined by subtracting from philosophy from photography, which means also subtracting every concern with the world or the real as philosophically determined. "Any philosophy of photography whatsoever—this is an invariant—will appeal to the World, to the perceived object, to perceiving subject," writes Laruelle.[8] Once photography is thought in terms of any of these positions—world, perceiving subject, or photographed object—then philosophy's capture is complete. So the problem for Laruelle is to think photography in entirely immanent terms. "The task of a rigorous thought" is "to found—at least in principle—an abstract theory of photography—but radically abstract, absolutely non-worldly and non-perceptual."[9] This then would be a theory—or at least a way of conceptually noting the possibility of a theory—of photography as such or what he calls the essence of the photo "in photo."[10]

The essence of the photograph is not to be found in what the photograph captures—neither in its reference nor in its indexicality—but in the *photograph as such* subtracted from any reference, referential function, or any philosophy that would organize these concepts. What appears in the photograph "is wholly distinct from the *photographic apparition* or from the representation of that object."[11] That which appears in the photograph is "wholly distinct" from the photographic reference presented. What appears is not just a photograph *of something* but the immanent photographical dimension or what Laruelle names the "immanent-being of the photo."[12] For Laruelle, this immanence of the photograph *qua* photograph is determined by the photographic "stance."

The mediating function of the camera (and of photography as a whole) cannot but take priority even if that is not the photographer's intention. When the body looks through a camera, it is rooted in a photographical orientation or stance. This stance or *body of photography* is not that of the "body with organs," notes Laruelle, with a nod to Deleuze and Guattari. This stance or body is undivided. Hand, eye, and torso are unified in a photographically choreographed gesture.

Laruelle writes:

> Before the eye, the hand, the torso are implicated in it, perhaps it is from the most obscure and most irreflexive depth of the body that the photographic act departs. Not from the organ-body or body as organ-support, from the substance-body, but from a body absolutely without organs, from a stance rather than from a position.[13]

The photographic "stance" is not that of the human body but of the body as formatted by photography. Before it is parceled out and *organ*ized into an anatomy of part-whole relations, there is this photographic essence as stance, as body of photography, undivided without organs. Prior to any philosophized set of relations—photographer-photography, camera-subject, position-perspective, subjective-objective—there is for Laruelle this always-already prior condition of photography *qua* stance. Stance "means: to be rooted in oneself," writes Laruelle, "to be held in one's own immanence, to be at one's station rather than in a position relative to the 'motif.'"[14]

The organizations and taxonomies of every philosophy of photography divide photography into technology, intentionality, reference, etc. All this is too philosophical or simply *is philosophical* for Laruelle. He seeks then a point of analysis prior to division that in its radical immanence suitably analogizes the real. Photography as stance prior to philosophical division functions here as the analog to the real as radical immanence prior to the scission of the real by philosophy. Laruelle writes:

> Photographic thought, rather than being primarily relational, differential, positional, is first of all real, in that sort of undivided experience, lived as non-positional self-vision-force, which has no need to posit itself with the World and to reflect itself in itself.[15]

Photographism names operations of Philosophical Decision that scission the real from philosophy. The "stance" of "non-photography" names the ideal comportment proper to all non-philosophical thought. Therefore, we have a clear opposition of two kinds of thought: photographism (philosophical taxonomy of the real) and non-photography (*qua* non-philosophical prioritization of the always-already prior immanence of the real).

Althusser's Photographism

Althusser's "theoretical theatre" is, I suggest, more like a suite of staged photographs: the cop, the hailing, the individual who turns (into a subject). These idealized freeze-frame shots present an imaginary image sequence of what is not in "reality" a sequence. Recall that Althusser's insists that ideology is "eternal." Althusser's "theoretical theatre" can be read then as a set of stilled images of what has always-already been—as if these scenes were always-already photographs. Schematically, Althusser's photo-theoretical theater is composed of a set of relations sequentially framed.

1. the street as setting
2. actors: cop and individual
3. action: cop's interpellation, hailing, turning of individual
4. the production of the subject

Each of these stilled frames presents the viewer-reader with a scene of something that has never been produced but only ever *reproduced*. It is precisely the opposite of what Roland Barthes identified as the indexical function of the photograph: it always says *this has been*.[16] Althusser's photographocentric logic says: *this (ideology) always-already has been*. Althusser's theory is an apparatus of framing and of presenting ideology as a sequence of images of what has always-already been. Here, I want to push an insight first developed with extraordinary dexterity in a lecture delivered by Philip Armstrong, which is thankfully archived online.[17]

Armstrong insightfully notes that the term "apparatus" is "*appareil*" in French. This word also marks the word for camera in French, "*appareil photo*." This, as Armstrong explains, is "both more and less" than a metaphorical coincidence. The whole question of the metaphor is a problematic around which the ISAs essay iteratively revolves. "The question at stake here," notes Armstrong, "becomes how the photographic comes to inscribe itself within the very terms of the text's argument." Armstrong's reading turns on "the rapport as such between the visibilities the apparatus brings into appearance and the conditions of visibility or exposure that inform Althusser's presentation of the ideological."[18]

The question of this rapport turns on the thematic of "reproducibility." The ISAs essay situates ideology as the answer to what secures the *"reproduction of the conditions of production."*[19] The question is: how to think the always-already logic of reproducibility? As Armstrong puts it, Althusser's guiding question demands a conceptualization of ideological "reproducibility" as something "constitutive of that phenomenon inscribed in and as its originary displacement."[20] In other words the photographocentric logic of the ISAs essay shows itself not merely as metaphor, but its argument attests to a central concern with the matter of reproducibility that, as Walter Benjamin showed long ago, is the logical core of photographic thinking.[21]

Althusser notes that Marx's theory of the State "makes it possible to inscribe in the theoretical apparatus of its essential concepts what I have called their respective *indices of effectivity*."[22] The conceptualization of a theory of ideology as necessarily a theory of State was inaugurated by Marx in the "theoretical apparatus" of *Capital*. Following Armstrong, what is crucial is that Marx's theory (and Marxist theory by extension) is also conceived as an apparatus or an *a-subjective machine of visibility* as Althusser conceptualizes it in *Reading Capital*. And, indeed, the very project of *Reading Capital* is itself a case of an apparatus of theory constructed to reproduce (by means of rereading) with a difference an apparatus of "scientific" thought in the name (if not manner) of Marx. Finally, Armstrong notes that Althusser organizes an optical and spatializing logic when he notes: "I shall call Ideological State Apparatuses a certain number of realities, which present themselves to the immediate observer."[23] The entire conception here of "realities" that "present" themselves to "the immediate observer" calls to mind a photographic encounter between the observer and the observed. But the terms "realities" and "immediate" are symptomatic. It signals a forgetting of the *mediated* nature of "seeing" and the mediated nature of (State) ideology as embodied in social institutions. Here we have an instance, in a sense, of what Benjamin calls the "optical unconscious"—a forgetting, in this case, of the fact that all acts of seeing are mediated—physiologically, psychically, and culturally.[24] The mediated nature of photographic seeing on this score is simply a hyper-visible instance of this fact. *The reality of seeing is reality as seen and this is never immediate but always mediated.* This is also true of that specific visibility constructed by theory as Althusser astutely (if enigmatically) notes. Althusser in *Reading Capital* writes:

> Any object or problem situated on the terrain and within the horizon, i.e., in the definite structured field of the theoretical problematic of a given theoretical discipline, is visible. We must take these words literally. The sighting is thus no longer the act of an individual subject, endowed with the faculty of "vision" which he exercises either attentively or distractedly: the sighting is the act of its structural conditions, it is the relation of immanent reflection between the field of the problematic and *its* objects and *its* problems.[25]

Theoretical sighting is an apparatus—an a-subjective machine—for producing visibilities. Like a camera lens, the theoretical "field" immanently constructs a zone of "reflection" between "the field of the [theoretical] problematic and *its* objects and *its* problems." This, I would argue, is not an instance of naive photographism but a *critical photographism*. The visibility of theory is here denoted as a highly mediated form of visibility immanently conditioned by the frame of a given theoretical problematic.

The ISAs essay by contrast denotes theory as an "apparatus" but it presents ideology as an immediate visibility for the reader. We might nuance the reading by suggesting that what Althusser has in mind is that ideology *appears* as immediate, but within the field of theory this appearance of immediacy is revealed to be mediated by ideological State apparatuses. But even if we go with this reading, then we still have to deal with the question of the apparatus of theory. This apparatus does not simply "reveal" what is the case nor does it simply "frame" ideology.

Rather, if we follow Althusser to the letter, then we must say that theory *produces* its object. In *Reading Capital*, Althusser insists that theory is not an extractive operation but a productive one. The "empiricist" theory of knowledge presumes that knowledge need only be "abstracted from real objects in the sense of an *extraction*," writes Althusser, as "gold is *extracted* ... from the dross of earth and sand in which it is held and contained."[26] This is precisely what Althusser rejects. Althusser writes, again in *Reading Capital*:

> While the production process of a given real object, a given real-concrete totality ... takes place entirely within the real and is carried out according to the real order of *real* genesis ... the production process of the object of knowledge takes place entirely within knowledge and is carried out according to a *different order*, in which thought categories which "reproduce" the real categories do *not* occupy *the same* place as they do in the order of the real historical genesis, but quite different places assigned them by their function in the production process of the object of knowledge.[27]

This is analogous to the relation of the photographed object to the "real" object. The photograph and that which it represents are fundamentally different. They belong to different orders. An apple and a photograph of an apple, for example, are materially distinct and the genesis of their production of course is also entirely different from one another. What appears in the photograph is (as Laruelle and Flusser show) a function of the theory of optics specific to a photographic technology (analog or digital). A detailed photograph can, like an adequate theory, "reproduce" its object by means of representation. But adequacy is not sameness. Here again Althusser evinces a *critical photographism* in his strict delineation between theoretical representation and the represented object itself.

But in the ISAs essay the difference between the two—between the theoretical representation of ideology and ideology as such—is obscured. And this forgetting of the mediated nature of theory symptomatically surfaces in the images of "real" figures and settings: the cop, the individual, the street. The elements of Althusser's "theoretical theatre" situate his theory within the images of the real rather than in the zone of immanent reflection governed by a given theoretical problematic.

Even if we put aside all this and simply assess the "rightness" of Althusser's theory then we encounter still another (and far more stubborn) obstacle. What does "rightness" mean in this context? Does it mean "adequacy?" No. It cannot mean anything like judging the accuracy of a photograph against its referent. Because in this case we cannot point "objectively" or "empirically" at ideology. One can index State apparatuses like the police, army, etc. But one cannot do the same for "ideology in general" or ideology as such precisely because this very formulation is not a direct index of the real of ideology but a model (an image) produced by the apparatus of theory, which is itself a model of what Althusser defines as a "representation of the imaginary relationship of individuals to their real conditions of existence."[28] Althusser's theory of ideology as subjection (the becoming-subject of the individual) is the becoming identified by (and with) an imaginary relationship to real conditions of existence.

Althusser's theory produces an object of knowledge: ideology as subjection to apparatuses of (State) power. But this by his own epistemological commitments cannot be a transcription of the "real" as the empiricist conception of knowledge has it. It must be a model produced by the apparatus of theory. Therefore, one can ask: what assures that this model is accurate or adequate to "real" ideology? Assessing its adequacy would require some knowledge of ideology as such that the model could then be compared to. But there is no empirical knowledge to be had of ideology as such. One can have empirical knowledge of the workings of State apparatuses such as the police and military, but such knowledge would not be *theoretical* knowledge of ideology. Althusser's theory of ideology is always-already a model or an image. We have then a peculiar photographism at this level: an immanent photographocentric model of ideology that refers to nothing empirical outside its theoreticist structure. To put this photographically, we have not a picture of something existing but of a reality that only exists photographically. We have then what Baudrillard would identify as a "simulacrum"—a *model without original.*

Philosophy as Capital

Laruelle counters naive theoretical photographism with a scientific and non-photographocentric thought. Laruelle proposes a *theory of theory* (like Althusser's) as a mode of production and not reflection. Laruelle's non-philosophical project is to establish a framework for the scientific investigation of the *ideology of philosophy*. At its core, this ideology manifests in the gesture of what Laruelle terms (often capitalized) "Philosophical Decision." Althusser theorizes ideology as the imaginary becoming-subject of the individual by subjection whereas Laruelle theorizes philosophy as the imaginary becoming-subject of the real by subjection to Philosophical Decision. *For Althusser there can be a scientific theory of ideology; for Laruelle there is only an ideology of philosophy that a science of philosophy alone can dispel.*

Laruelle's commitment to Marx is clear. But equally so is his criticism of Marxism (qua standard philosophy). In *Introduction to Non-Marxism*, Laruelle challenges Marxist philosophy by voiding it of the proletariat as unitary image. Whereas Althusser does philosophy *for Marx*, Laruelle radicalizes Marx's oft-repeated quips about the need to transcend philosophy. A key passage sums up much of what Laruelle means by "non-Marxism." Responding to the long history of returns to and revisions of Marx (including that by Althusser), Laruelle writes:

> We do not oppose a doctrinal regression to these philosophically saturated forms, or a withdrawal, or a step back into the undetermined of the unthought, but rather *a non-Marxist practice of Marxism* is destined to struggle against the "particular interests" of philosophical systems desperately attempting to capture it, and this can already be seen in Marx's work. The error would be believing that the suspension of these philosophical postulates, the suspension of the postulate of philosophy itself, insofar as it tries to and believes itself capable of determining Marxism, amounts to a regression into economism, into a thoughtless and vulgar Marxism.[29]

Non-Marxism (or non-standard Marxism) aims to strip away the vested "interests" by careerist proponents and more so by reactionary opportunists. Laruelle, like Marx, attacks philosophy because he sees its standard practice as coterminous with the logic of capital. I explored this in a recent book—*The Real Is Radical*—where I contend that Laruelle targets the intertwined logic of exchange and equivalence of capital. As money is a "universal equivalent" so concepts operate in standard knowledge economies as "equivalents" for the real.[30] It is not merely that there is analogy between conceptual economies of knowledge and monetary economic structures.

Laruelle argues that *capital is a philosophy* (as Marx knew) complete with its own literature beset by what Marx famously called its "theological niceties." Non-Marxism is a call to think from a an-economic and decommodified standpoint. Non-philosophy refuses the lure of philosophy to pose as the medium of exchange for thought and the real. Marxism in this form would then refuse to operationalize the exchange-equivalence logic endemic to capitalism as philosophy. The "object of non-Marxism," writes Laruelle, "will be capitalism plus the set, structured in 'essence,' of its philosophical conditions, meaning 'universal' capitalism."[31] Global capitalism today has only further ramified the ideology that capitalism is the universal (and universally good) form of social order. And it is precisely this that Laruelle calls into question.

Every term of traditional Marxism, such as the "proletariat" or "labor power," is reformatted by Laruelle in a way that disenables its economic-philosophical dimension. For example, of labor power, Laruelle writes that non-Marxism operates by "treating it as a symptom of a new kind, as a structure inadmissible in the combined terms of economy (of capitalism) and philosophy."[32] Laruelle will hold onto the concept of power (or "force"). According to Laruelle, a theory of political force that stems from the presupposed primacy of labor always-already affirms the primacy of the economy and is therefore philosophically allied to capitalist thought. Laruelle subtracts the concept "labor" from his project in order to recast resistance outside the logic of capital without excluding practices of anti-capitalist resistance. Laruelle opts for a generic model of struggle. "Being a practical subject of struggle," writes Laruelle, "only as a subject constituted within the immanence of the *in-struggle* or the struggle that we will call 'uni-class.'"[33] Laruelle parallels the concerns of many post-Marxists in his interest to move Marxist discourse beyond a concern for the search for the univocal subject of history in the form of the working-class proletariat.

Laruelle writes:

> What ... Marxist name can we give the ... subject-(of)-struggle, who *is* in-struggle in an immanent way? Proletariat? Plebe? Ordinary man? Minorities? People? Excluded? All these terms can be utilized under the general conditions of the theoretical re-treatment that non-Marxism is. Nevertheless, one of them is more

rigorous through its axiomatic character, of course, we mean the "non-proletariat."[34]

Laruelle writes "universal" as "uni-versal" to underscore his axiomatic insistence that the real "acts" unilaterally—traversing in one direction. Struggle is "in" the real as is philosophy. They are never autonomous and are conditioned in the last instance by it. Laruelle's "theoretical re-treatment" of Marxism recasts it as a politics of force against the hegemony of speculation (financial and standard philosophical thinking alike). Laruelle's retreatment of Marxism somewhat parallels Rancière's critique of Althusser's erasure of class struggle. But Laruelle goes one move further by eliminating "class" (conceptualized economically) in favor of placing primacy on struggle generically conceived. Here it is worth noting that whereas, for Althusser, the very concept of the "subject" signifies subjection, for Laruelle, the subject is always a site of struggle and is indeed formed "in-struggle."

Photo-Fiction

In *Photo-Fiction, a Non-standard Aesthetics*, Laruelle expands on and revises some of his initial formulations on non-photography. Here he appeals to an anti-mimetic, non-photographocentric thinking on the model of what he calls "fiction." Non-philosophy is here envisioned as a radically abstract (almost iconophobic) procedure of fictionalization. Laruelle writes:

> Thus, neither photographer nor aesthetician, what am I doing here? I'm not doing aesthetics but trying to build a thought that exceeds or replaces the general process of philosophical aesthetics and its descriptions. This is a practice of a quite special genre that is not completely standard or recognized. It would be a bit like an artisan, to use a Socratic example, who instead of making a bed following the ideal model of a bed ... got in his head to make an Idea of the

bed that would somewhat resemble the bed but which would also not be its copy, but rather a "generic" extension of the bed.[35]

Non-photographic (or non-philosophical) thought does not seek to capture, copy, or transcribe a model. It is a procedure for reimagining the imaginative and creative powers of theory. It is an artisanal process of creative making not governed by the real but not irrelevant to it any more than literature is to reality. The practice of non-philosophy in a non-photographocentric register is a "new genre" of thinking that presumes a radical insufficiency with respect to the real but which nonetheless affirms its immanent determination by it in the last instance. Laruelle continues:

> This photo-fictional theoretical apparatus ... is probably not made for taking pictures to put into albums or the more modern methods of viewing photos, it is made only for generating fictions that are like "theoretical captions" ... Let us invert the Platonic relation of Ideas and the objects that copy them, let us take this object ... and treat it as a model in the sense of a model for an axiomatic without making another model in the Platonic sense.[36]

Photo-fiction is not about capturing and captioning the real. It is a practice not of modeling the real (of the Idea, of the World, politics, art, etc.), but of taking that very idea as an object of study. Photo-fiction captures the standard ideology of philosophical capture in a non-imagistic register. Non-Marxism understood as "photo-fiction" is a radically non-representationalist practice of Marxist theory. There are two poles in Laruelle's non-photographocentric Marxist practice: a non-representationalist imperative with respect to the real and a representationalist imperative to capture philosophy's decisionist pseudo-capture of the real. Non-philosophy takes a picture of philosophy's picture-taking-like claims on the real. The point is not to pierce the illusionary caprice of photographocentric philosophy only. It is rather to radicalize a metacritical perspective that accounts for the constructed nature of photographocentric discourse precisely in order to more fully exploit its capacity to create. "Non-standard aesthetics is creative and inventive and its genre is that of philo-fiction," writes Laruelle, "a philosophical artistic genre that strives to make a work with pure and abstract thought."[37]

Laruelle's conception of theory as fiction has two immediate consequences. First, it calls for the practice of theory as a genre not as a neutral analysis of reality much less the real. But it also implies that this is how we should read *all theory* as a genre of writing. The practice of theory is a practice of a certain writing. On this model, much could be nominated as theory from novels to visual works of art to many other forms of writing that refuse easy categorization. This means taking much more seriously than Althusser seems to the metaphorical investments that underwrite the ISAs essay. Althusser's metaphors construct a photographocentric frame of operation that theoretically freeze-frames the concept of ideology. This frame converts the idea of ideology in general into a specific sequence of images: the street, the cop, the hailed subject.

Aesthetic Ideology

Althusser's theory, seen by Laruelle's lights, is part of a genealogy of theories of ideology (and the unconscious) that rely upon images (often which their writers disavow). Consider Freud's comment in *Interpretation of Dreams* that the work of the unconscious may be likened to the development of photographic negatives: the unconscious as a "photographic apparatus."[38] Or, as noted in Chapter 1, Marx's metaphor of ideology as a "camera obscura" in which reality appears as a dematerialized spectacle composed of free-floating values, ideas, beliefs, etc.

Althusser's essay has its place in this complex genealogy of attempts to think the conditions of subject formation by means of metaphors that their authors attempt to hold at bay.

To be clear: I don't think it is right to reduce theory and literature to some supra-category. There are differences between theory and fiction. But the problem is how to draw those distinctions. To begin with it is not at all clear which field should (if any) draw the line. Is this a question for literature or theory? Who or what owns the right to draw that line. Some might care to draw the line between the forms of knowledge demarcated by each field. Theory is concerned with the production of knowledge and the status of knowledge itself and is therefore an "epistemological" discipline. The arts deal in the realm of the aesthetic. But this relies on a quite dated conception of art as tied to the matter of aesthetic experience, which entirely rules out a good deal of modern and contemporary art that challenges that linkage and lineage. Indeed, the very notion of "the aesthetic" as a category is itself the product of modernist epistemological practices that aimed to identify and isolate this aspect of experience. The philosophical ideal of "the aesthetic" as an autonomous category of experience is by no means given or natural. It belongs to a certain philosophical ideology of "experience" deeply indebted to a modern conception of culture as something composed of discrete spheres: the public, the private, the economic, the political, the aesthetic, etc. Althusser as a good Marxist rightly rejects this model. Society can be *analyzed* discretely, but it operates as an overdetermined structural totality. And yet, on at least one occasion, Althusser defaulted into the bourgeois ideology of separate spheres. In his "A Letter on Art in Reply to André Daspre," he affirms the division of labor between art and knowledge. He writes:

> Art (I mean authentic art, not works of average or mediocre level) does not replace *knowledge* in the *strict sense*, it therefore does not replace knowledge (in the modern sense: scientific knowledge),

> but what it gives us does maintain a certain *specific relationship* with knowledge. This relationship is not one of identity but one of difference. Let me explain. I believe that a peculiarity of art is to "make us see" ... "make us perceive," "make us feel" something which alludes reality. ... What art makes us *see*, and therefore gives to us in the form of "*seeing*," "*perceiving*" and "*feeling*" (which is not the form of knowing), is the *ideology* from which it is born, in which it bathes, from which it detaches itself as art, and which it *alludes*.[39]

Althusser distinguishes between scientific theory as knowledge in the "strict sense" from art which only has "specific relationship with knowledge." Art allows us to see, perceive, and feel the "ideology from which it is born" and in which it (like all of us) "bathes." Art (at least "authentic art") "detaches" itself from the ideology of which it is born and by this detachment shows the ideology from which it came. As the navel marks the detachment of the body from its mother, so art is marked by its detachment from the ideology that birthed it. But this "specific relationship" of detachment does not qualify as knowledge according to Althusser.

Althusser affirms the distinction between the epistemological and the aesthetic. Art enables us to "see," "perceive," and "feel"—it enables aesthetic experience—but it does not furnish knowledge. But, of course, this very distinction between aesthetic experience and knowledge is itself a theoretical postulate. The line between the epistemological (knowledge) and the aesthetic (experience) is drawn by philosophy. Althusser affirms this ideology by operationalizing precisely what Laruelle terms the Philosophical Decision: the decision on *the real nature of knowledge*. This decision arrogates to philosophy the supremacy of its own definition of knowledge to the exclusion of all others. But the metaphorical dimension of Althusser's Philosophical Decision troubles the very demarcation he draws.

The tropological structure of "birth"—"born," "detachment," "bathes"—enables us (readers) to "see," "perceive," and perhaps even "feel" Althusser's point, but in so doing it deconstructs his line of demarcation between "the aesthetic" and "knowledge in the strict sense." Althusser's trouble with metaphors is an object lesson in what Paul de Man in the "The Epistemology of Metaphor" argues is endemic to all philosophy. The "relationship and the distinction between literature and philosophy," writes de Man, "cannot be made in terms of a distinction between aesthetic and epistemological categories. All philosophy is condemned, to the extent that it is dependent on figuration, to be literary and, as the depository of this very problem, all literature is to some extent philosophical."[40] De Man's point is not that there are no differences between philosophy and literature. Rather the distinction always raises a difficult question: what (if anything) stabilizes the distinction? Epistemology and aesthetics are bound up with one another because materially speaking philosophy is a form (or forms) of writing and as such is bound up with metaphors, images, analogies, and other literary tropes.

The philosophical and the aesthetic continually cross-contaminate one another's domains. What de Man identifies as "aesthetic ideology" is precisely the attempt by philosophy to distinguish philosophy and literature and thereby preserve the possibility of rigorous aesthetic theory. Philosophy attempts to keep "the aesthetic" in its place precisely by delimiting the supposed existence of the autonomy of "the aesthetic." "Metaphors, tropes, and figural language in general have been a perennial problem," writes de Man, "and by extension for all discursive uses of language including historiography and literary analysis."[41] Figural language haunts the epistemological aims of historiography, literary analysis, and one might add, art history and theory, for the same reason it haunts philosophy. It troubles the line between analysis and object of analysis. It follows that the practice of historiography, literary analysis, art history and theory, and all humanities study is "philosophical" in Laruelle's sense in that it attempts to operationalize the Philosophical Decision of scission between philosophy and art. De Man continues:

> It appears that philosophy either has to give up its own constitutive claim to rigor in order to come to terms with the figurality of its language or that it has to free itself from figuration altogether. And if the latter is considered impossible, philosophy could at least learn to control figuration by keeping it, so to speak, in its place, by delimiting the boundaries of its influence and thus restricting the epistemological damage that it may cause.[42]

De Man here strikes to my ear at least a decidedly Laruellian and Rancièrian tone. Philosophy on this reading is a policing figure that delimits the boundaries of figurality in order to protect its rule of/over knowledge. Philosophy here is figured as an authority figure—even an authoritarian figure—who rules on the question of what counts as knowledge in the "strict sense" in order to preserve its epistemological monopolization and subject all other forms of knowledge to its border controls. Philosophy works to secure the border between the epistemological and the aesthetic by apprehending illicit border crossers.

Science of Philosophy

Whereas Althusser's post-theoreticist phase—beginning with "Lenin and Philosophy"—militantly reorients the authority of philosophy by submitting it to the dictates of class struggle, Laruelle militantly orients his project against philosophical authoritarianism. And whereas Althusser rallies philosophical science to defend materialism, Laruelle marshals a "science of philosophy" to subject philosophy to ruthless critique. Both projects can cite Marx's authority. Althusser's Marx is the Marx of *Capital*; Laruelle's Marx is that of "Theses on Feuerbach."

"Science" is the determining term for each. But Althusser's "science" is determined by philosophy. Laruelle's by contrast is "science" *de-determined* by philosophy (*qua* Philosophical Decision). The confrontation between Althusser and Laruelle staged here is not that between theory and a simplistic post-philosophical embrace of science. The irony of today's anti-philosophy science popularizers is that they just do philosophy badly. Claims that science has gone beyond philosophy usually end up somewhere on the far side of metaphysics to put it nicely. Non-philosophy isn't that. It is a theory. Non-philosophy "produces *theoretical* and no longer *philosophical* thought," writes Laruelle.[43] It constructs its object of knowledge theoretically: the object of knowledge called "philosophy." In *Theory of Identities*, Laruelle notes:

> Non-philosophy ... seeks to be "scientific" in its method and its essence, but immediately touches on philosophy in its object. It strives to extend the criteria of scientific thought, which is rethought beforehand in its autonomy, to the theory and practice of philosophy. But it is not in any way a mode of "philosophy as rigorous science" or the negation of philosophy. It is a positive, autonomous discipline, which aims to inscribe itself in the lineage of sciences while rectifying their epistemological concept. It proceeds through operations of the type "experimentation" and "deduction." But, on the one hand, it remains transcendental and nonpositivist (hence its other possible designations: "transcendental science" or "first science") and, on the other, it applies its operations to philosophical statements, thus to "natural" and not logically formalized language.[44]

Non-philosophy takes philosophical materials as its object of study, but it transforms them into an object of knowledge through theoretical practices of deduction and experimentation. It is therefore not solely an analytical practice. Its aim is to analyze the general functioning of philosophical systems. But it also aims to decompose those systems into material resources for experiments in non-decisionist modes of thought production. Non-philosophy as science of philosophy is a positive discipline in that it has positive content, namely philosophical materials and Philosophical Decisions. But it is also "transcendental" and "nonpositivist" in that the material it works on (philosophical materials) is transformed into non-philosophical material.

This material is the object of a "science of a new type," writes Laruelle, "not extracted from philosophical mixtures, but globally anterior to them."[45] Non-philosophical practice releases itself from the grip of philosophical concern for the "real" and deals instead with the logic and effects of philosophical materials. It does not concern itself with deciding which philosophy is right with respect to the real for that is precisely a *philosophical* problem. Rather, it is concerned to interrogate the specific ways that standard philosophy carries out Philosophical Decisions.

Laruelle writes:

> We will call this discipline [of non-philosophy] *transcendental* or *first science*; by its material (philosophy) and its product (non-philosophy in the strict sense of the term) ... This term and its "non-Euclidian" analogy make it sufficiently clear that it is not a matter of negating philosophy or "leaving" it—impossible operations—but of recognizing that its alleged validity and its claims over the real have always been suspended by science.[46]

Good scientific practice does not assume that there is a real of the phenomenon to be known apart from what it can observe and model. And that is its power. It remains open to knowledge because it does not arbitrarily assume a closed or unitary real of phenomena in the first place.

Non-philosophy as science of philosophy likewise suspends any concern with the real. Its object is not "ultimate reality" but the material reality of philosophy (broadly defined) and its effects. The material of non-philosophy is the immanent mechanisms, institutional dynamics, and social and political effects of philosophical hegemony. Philosophical Decision (or statements to that effect) delimits the scope of non-philosophy. For, as Laruelle notes, "such a science would have no sense, at least as a theory, if it did not let itself be determined—within some precise [axiomatic] limits—by philosophy as well as by its material."[47] Non-philosophy is a science of philosophical materials. But in constructing this object of knowledge (philosophy and its decisionist dynamics), non-philosophy also voids philosophy of the very authority it operationalizes by its standard decisionist orientation.

No Pictures

Non-philosophy as science of philosophy is arguably given its most concrete formulation in Laruelle's *Theory of Identities*. But like most of Laruelle's texts, this text is a kind of theoretical preface to a practice to come. Laruelle's major texts hardly ever show, with rare exceptions, what in practice non-philosophy would look like. This reticence to show us what non-philosophy looks like in practice stems from a kind of iconophobic impulse in Laruelle's writing which mitigates against the chance of defaulting back into a photographocentric form of thought.

Laruelle instead *images philosophical imaging* itself. He tries to *show philosophical showing* without indexing anything visual or otherwise capturable which would only operationalize and affirm philosophical capture.

Non-philosophy's ban on images marks most of Laruelle's work not least of all *Introduction to Non-Marxism*. Ian James in a review of that book notes something that applies to any of Laruelle's major texts. Non-philosophy's radicality lies in its "ambition to be a non-representational style of theory."⁴⁸ Laruelle's work aims toward a radical "formalism," notes James, insofar as it "describe[s] or represent[s] absolutely nothing of the invisible Real."⁴⁹ Indeed, a chapter on Laruelle could have fit very well into Martin Jay's book, *Downcast Eyes: The Denigration of Vision in Twentieth-Century French Thought*. Jay argues that many French thinkers of the twentieth century (including Althusser) evinced an interest in vision and visuality and a profound suspicion of its hold on the philosophical imagination. "Although definitions of visuality vary from thinker to thinker," writes Jay, "it is clear that occularcentrism aroused (and continues to arouse) a widely shared distrust."⁵⁰ Vision for thinkers such as Guy Debord and Michel Foucault (to name just two) is a figure of distrust because it is linked to apparatuses of capture and domination such as the thrall of the spectacle (Debord) or the imprisoning glare of the panopticon (Foucault). Althusser and Laruelle both engage in considerations of vision—think of Laruelle's writings on photography or Althusser on painting—still each remains suspicious, the latter even more so, of the link between vision and thought. But this does make reading Laruelle difficult because he indexes without imaging. He points not at something so much as at philosophical indexation itself. He seeks a non-philosophical science of philosophy that would capture philosophical statements voided of their indexical claim on the real. As James notes:

> The notion of adequation here is decisive: such a theory would not strictly speaking be a simple representation of the Real *as* unrepresentable, nor would it be a negative knowledge of the Real by way of apophatic saying. Rather it would be a theory that seeks to make itself adequate to the unrepresentable Real by divesting itself of all vestigial traces of representational logic.⁵¹

Non-philosophy is a critique of the representational logic of all standard philosophy and therefore by extension all standard philosophies of ideology. But it makes this critique by the logic of non-representation itself. Laruelle does not go in for a direct engagement with a specific philosophy—no snapshots of philosophies or much in the way of direct citational practice—so much as indexing the means by which standard philosophy cannot sever itself from being an index of something it nominates as the "real." Non-philosophy is a form of critique that does not image the object of that critique. Instead, it works by means of a rigorous formalism—the terms of which are "real," "Philosophical Decision," "philo-fiction," "non-philosophy," and others.

These terms constitute the grammar of its formal operations. But rarely will Laruelle provide discretely finished models or images of what non-philosophy looks (or is supposed to look) like. His texts are often presented as "introductions" or prefatory gestures for non-philosophy. He refuses to image non-philosophy and thereby preserves his project's anti-mimeticism. In this sense, we might also say that Laruelle marks a decisive intervention in the history of "post-criticism" as defined by Ulmer.

The formal grammar of non-philosophy is designed *to point at philosophical pointing*. Katerina Kolozova notes that in this respect non-philosophy "consists of transcendental material of 'theoretico-technico-experimental ingredients'" that enable the transformation of this material into something non-philosophical or "philo-fictional" in character.[52] Philosophical material is transcendentalized by suspending its claim on the real and thereby liberating it from its systematic dependence on what it hallucinates as its real object. All that remains of philosophy as a consequence of this transcendentalizing operation is a unitary structure of decision. "Since, according to Laruelle, the ... [mixture] of thought, the real, and thought's self-sufficiency determine philosophy in the last instance," writes Kolozova, "one can speak of philosophy in a scientific theory ... but not necessarily of the philosophy canonically identified as such."[53] Non-philosophy defines "philosophy" not by philosophical content but by its decisionist imperative with respect to the real. From the standpoint of non-philosophy, philosophy is an object of knowledge, not a repository of knowledge of the real.

To conclude, we can see that whereas Althusser wants a general theory of ideology, Laruelle wants a general theory of philosophy. Both invoke science as a means to accomplish these ends even though how science is defined in both projects marks the site of their radical divergence. Whereas Althusser seeks to define ideology as subjection to the rule of the idea of the subject, Laruelle identifies philosophy itself as so many operations of subjection. All philosophies of the form "*philosophy of*" (philosophy of art, philosophy of politics, philosophy of ideology, etc.) syntactically and epistemologically subordinate one field of knowledge or practice to the dictates of philosophy. All philosophy makes subjects out of its others. And in this respect, Laruelle affirms Althusser's linkage—ideology = subjection—but he turns it back on philosophy broadly defined and calls for an emancipatory resistance against its authority and indeed authoritarianism.

Notes

1. Althusser, *For Marx*, 113.
2. Laruelle, *The Concept of Non-photography*, trans. Robin Mackay (New York: Urbanomic/Sequence Press, 2012), 2.
3. Vilém Flusser, *Towards a Philosophy of Photography*, trans. Anthony Mathews (London: Reaktion Books, 2012), 41–2.
4. Laruelle, *The Concept of Non-photography*, 2.
5. Ibid., 4.
6. Ibid.
7. Ibid.
8. Ibid., 3.
9. Ibid., 8.
10. Ibid., 50.
11. Ibid., 18.

12 Ibid., 20.
13 Ibid., 12.
14 Ibid.
15 Ibid., 12–13.
16 Roland Barthes, *Camera Lucida: Reflections on Photography*, trans. Richard Howard (New York: Hill and Wang, 2010).
17 Philip Armstrong, "Scenes of Interpellation," https://www.youtube.com/watch?v=7rxn1nYWcbU&t=159s.
18 Ibid.
19 Althusser, "Ideology and Ideological State Apparatuses," 85.
20 Armstrong, "Scenes of Interpellation."
21 See Walter Benjamin, "The Work of Art in the Age of Its Technological Reproducibility," in *The Work of Art in the Age of Its Technological Reproducibility and Other Writings on Media*, trans. Edmund Jephcott, et al. (Cambridge: Belknap Press of Harvard University, 2008).
22 Althusser, "Ideology and Ideological State Apparatuses," 90.
23 Ibid., 96.
24 Walter Benjamin, "The Work of Art in the Age of Its Technological Reproducibility," 37.
25 Althusser, *Reading Capital*, 24.
26 Ibid., 35.
27 Ibid., 41.
28 Althusser, "Ideology and Ideological State Apparatuses," 109.
29 François Laruelle, *Introduction to Non-Marxism*, trans. Anthony Paul Smith (Minneapolis: Univocal Publishing, 2015), 3.
30 See Jonathan Fardy, *The Real Is Radical: Marx after Laruelle* (London: Bloomsbury Academic, 2022).
31 Laruelle, *Introduction to Non-Marxism*, 5.
32 Ibid., 126.
33 Ibid., 132.
34 Ibid.
35 François Laruelle, *Photo-Fiction, a Non-standard Aesthetics*, trans. Drew S. Burk (Minneapolis: Univocal Publishing, 2012), 12.

36 Ibid., 12–13.
37 Ibid., 6.
38 Sigmund Freud, *The Interpretation of Dreams*, trans. James Strachey (London: Penguin, 1976), 686.
39 Louis Althusser, "A Letter on Art in Reply to André Daspre," in *Lenin and Philosophy and Other Essays*, 152.
40 Paul de Man, *Aesthetic Ideology* (Minneapolis: University of Minnesota Press, 1996), 50.
41 Ibid., 34.
42 Ibid.
43 François Laruelle, *Theory of Identities*, trans. Alyosha Edlebi (New York: Columbia University Press, 2016), 82.
44 Ibid., 79.
45 Ibid., 21.
46 Ibid., 82.
47 Ibid.
48 Ian James, "Review of *Introduction to Non-Marxism*," *Notre Dame Philosophical Reviews*, December 12, 2013, https://ndpr.nd.edu/reviews/introduction-to-non-marxism/.
49 Ibid.
50 Martin Jay, *Downcast Eyes: The Denigration of Vision in Twentieth-Century French Thought* (Berkeley: University of California Press, 1994), 588.
51 James, "Review of *Introduction to Non-Marxism*."
52 Katerina Kolozova, *Capitalism's Holocaust of Animals: A Non-Marxist Critique of Capital, Philosophy, and Patriarchy* (London: Bloomsbury Academic, 2020), 61.
53 Katerina Kolozova, *Toward a Radical Metaphysics of Socialism: Marx and Laruelle* (Brooklyn: Punctum Books, 2015), 6.

7

Conclusion

The commonplace that postwar theory amounts to the dissolution of the concept of the subject is belied by the work of Althusser, Rancière, Baudrillard, and Laruelle who rather put the subject in question. To question is not to dissolve. Indeed, it is to reanimate anew with a difference. Precisely because it had *become a question*, the subject could be reformulated in the most rigorously anti-humanist terms stripped of liberal-humanist ideological mystifications.

Chapter 2 examined the historical elements of Althusser's theory of ideology. We began with Marx's concept of "commodity fetishism." This concept spawned two schools of thought in theories of ideology. One school considers ideology to be false consciousness (á la Lukács). The other, which Althusser affirms, treats consciousness—and all philosophies from empiricism to phenomenology that are based on it—as itself symptomatic of liberal-humanist ideology. This line of thought has its roots in the work of Cavaillès who coined the term "philosophy of the concept" in opposition to all philosophies of consciousness. We noted that Althusser's militantly anti-humanist epistemology is through and through a political project to beat back the creeping liberalism initiated by the de-Stalinization of the CPSU. Finally, we noted that "theory" in the theoreticist orientation functions as a kind of stand-in for the agency of the subject.

Chapter 3 looked to how Althusser's political ban on talk of the subject came to be contested by students who looked East to reformulate a theory of the subject along the lines of the Maoist militant. We examined Althusser's highly ambivalent reaction to this development. On the one hand he praises Mao but denies his work any real theoretical significance. He instead insists that the Cultural Revolution can (and should) be read in terms established by the science of Marxism-Leninism. We then looked at students and young thinkers such as Badiou and others who saw in Maoism the practice and theory of a new form of revolutionary subjectivity. Looking also to the contemporary work of Pang, we noted how the disparaging view of French Maoism, epitomized by Wolin, can be corrected by a more nuanced understanding of Maoist aesthetics and a critical rejection of "cult of personality" as pseudo-concept (something that Althusser also affirms). The chapter concluded with an examination of Althusser's theory of ideology.

Specifically, we focused on Althusser's attempt to have done with a conception of ideology as false consciousness and instead to root the concept in a materialist frame based on material institutions. We noted Althusser's trouble with metaphors, specifically temporal metaphors, which undermine his claim that "ideology has no history." We saw how the scene of interpellation opens up three avenues of research addressed by each of our subsequent three thinkers: the ideology of intellectual vanguardism (Rancière), the problem of form in theoretical construction (Baudrillard), and the ideology of philosophy (Laruelle).

Chapter 4 looked at Rancière's break with Althusser and his turn to the archives of working-class protest in nineteenth-century France. We examined first the roots of his theoretical break. These lie in his conviction that Althusserianism reproduces the division of labor between intellectual and manual work. Thinkers think and workers should do what thinkers say. What he found in the archives were stories of workers who refused the interpellative solicitations of work and work-centric politics. They embodied a practical and oneiric protest for another kind of work: philosophical and poetic production and enjoyment freed from the wage form. Rancière's historiographic interventions realized a "logical revolt" in standard Marxist historiographies of the working class. His studies revealed the existence of the "empirical proletariat" for whom the question was not how to improve work but how to have done with work itself. The archive revealed that the empirical proletariat had never needed the secrets of ideological domination explained to them. They didn't need Marxist science, but the revolt for which Marxist politics ought to stand. Finally, we examined Rancière's work on the history of the working class against work in light of workerist thought and action then on the march in Italy. Seen in light of the development of Italian workerism we can grasp the contemporaneity of Rancière's nineteenth-century historiography. Rancière and workerism challenge the intellectual-manual division of labor and with it the entire tradition of Marxian theoretical vanguardism. Both exposed the ideological dimension of that tradition.

Chapter 5 examined the work of Baudrillard. Specifically, we interrogated his continuing fidelity to a certain conception of ideology critique in his theory of the simulacrum. Baudrillard's work follows in the Althusserian wake in a peculiar sense. For Althusser, the subject is produced by an object: the machine of State ideological apparatuses. For Baudrillard, the issue for theory is to think the object as such apart from any concept of the subject since that has now "become untenable." This takes the form of a certain literary style in Baudrillard's work that exemplifies an entire movement in the late 1960s through the 1970s in which conceptual artists, such as Kosuth, and theorists, such as Derrida, attempted to objectify the written word so as to turn writing into an objectal form. While Baudrillard's work is a good example of what Ulmer long ago identified as "post-criticism," we also noted that it is haunted (à la Derrida) by the spirit of the subject of critique of old. Finally, we noted how Baudrillard's turn to the object parallels Althusser's concern with the material object of ideology. Ideology for Althusser is embodied in institutional objects and theory itself in his works of 1965 is understood as a "field," an object, then, which makes visible problems by means of theoretical "reflections" immanently generated by the theoretical field and "its object and its problems."

Chapter 6 examined Laruelle's critique of the ideology of "standard philosophy." Laruelle identifies a "photographocentric" bias in "standard" philosophy. Laruelle argues that philosophy and photography (in their standard practices and theoretical images) have been tied to the ideology of the capture of the "real." Laruelle counters by treating photography as a technology that *produces a specifically photographic real*. Laruelle sees standard philosophy in the same way. It does not reflect the real. It produces its image (or an hallucination of it) by means of what Laruelle terms "Philosophical Decision."

A photographocentric bias can be detected in Althusser's ISAs essay. The essay's reliance on photographocentric metaphors ramified by metaphors of reproducibility reveals a desire to capture an image (or instance) of ideology. But this desire betrays the putative aims of the essay, namely not to theorize specific instances of ideology *but ideology in general*. We then turned to Laruelle's rewriting of Marxism in the form of a radically nonrepresentational "photo-fiction" or "philo-fiction." I then attempted to develop Laruelle's insights by turning to a critique of Althusser's apparent distinction between the "philosophical" or "theoretical" and the "aesthetic." This distinction is precisely what de Man identifies as "aesthetic ideology." How then to escape this aesthetic ideology? Laruelle's answer is no longer to draw lines of demarcation between science (determined philosophically) and ideology but rather to subject philosophy to a new kind of science voided of philosophical decisionism: a science of philosophy. The object of this science of philosophy is the decisionist imperative of philosophy and its effects. Laruelle in this sense follows Althusser: he holds firmly to a conception of theoretical work as productive and never as mere capture. But whereas Althusser wants a general theory of ideology, Laruelle wants a general non-philosophical theory of standard philosophy.

My aim throughout these chapters has been to trace the origins and legacies of theories of ideology as interpellation. My constellation of thinkers answers the theoretical necessity to recast the theory of ideology not as the problem of consciousness but that of structures (Althusser), history (Rancière), objectality (Baudrillard), and philosophy itself (Laruelle). Their work begins not with the subject as such but with the subject as problem, question, and terrain of contestation. Their work demonstrates the necessity of theory as epistemological resource and political battleground. Collectively, it offers a powerful riposte to all those who celebrate the "death of theory," which is so often nothing more than the palest of ideologies.

Bibliography

Adorno, Theodor and Max Horkheimer. *Dialectic of Enlightenment: Philosophical Fragments*, edited by Gunzellin Schmid Noerr, translated by Edmund Jephcott. Stanford: Stanford University Press, 2007.

Althusser, Louis. *Essays in Self-Criticism*, translated by Grahame Lock. London: NLB, 1976.

Althusser, Louis. *For Marx*, translated by Ben Brewster. New York: Vintage, 1969.

Althusser, Louis. *Lenin and Philosophy and Other Essays*, translated by Ben Brewster. New York: Monthly Review Press, 2001.

Althusser, Louis. "On Cultural Revolution," translated by Jason Smith. *Decalages*, Vol. 1, No. 1 (2014). https://progressivegeographies.com/2013/12/29/althussers-1966-piece-on-the-chinese-cultural-revolution/.

Althusser, Louis. *Philosophy and the Spontaneous Philosophy of the Scientists*, edited by Gregory Elliott, translated by Ben Brewster, et al. London: Verso, 2011.

Althusser, Louis. *Reading Capital: The Complete Edition*, translated by Ben Brewster and David Fernbach. London: Verso, 2015.

Althusser, Louis. *The Humanist Controversy and Other Writings (1966–67)*, edited by François Matheron, translated by G. M. Goshgarian. London: Verso, 2003.

Armstrong, Philip. "Scenes of Interpellation." https://www.youtube.com/watch?v=7rxn1nYWcbU&t=159s.

Badiou, Alain. "The Althusserian Definition of 'Theory.'" In *The Concept in Crisis: Reading Capital Today*, edited by Nick Nesbitt, 21–34. Durham: Duke University Press, 2017.

Badiou, Alain. *The Communist Hypothesis*, translated by David Macey and Steven Corcoran. London: Verso, 2010.

Badiou, Alain. *Theory of the Subject*, translated by Bruno Bosteels. London: Bloomsbury Academic, 2013.

Balestrini, Nanni. *We Want Everything*, translated by Matt Holden. London: Verso, 2016.

Bargu, Banu. "Althusser's Materialist Theater: Ideology and Its Aporias." *Differences: A Journal of Feminist and Cultural Studies*, Vol. 26, No. 3 (2015): 81–106.

Barthes, Roland. *Camera Lucida: Reflections on Photography*, translated by Richard Howard. New York: Hill and Wang, 2010.

Baudrillard, Jean. *Fatal Strategies*, translated by Philippe Beitchman and W. G. J. Nielsluchowski. Los Angeles: Semiotext(e), 2008.

Baudrillard, Jean. *Forget Foucault*. New York: Semiotext(e), 1987.

Baudrillard, Jean. *In the Shadow of the Silent Majorities, or The End of the Social, and Other Essays*, translated by Paul Patton, et al. New York: Semiotext(e), 1983.

Baudrillard, Jean. *Simulations*, translated by Paul Foss, et al. New York: Semiotext(e), 1983.

Baudrillard, Jean. *The Intelligence of Evil or The Lucidity Pact*, translated by Chris Turner. London: Bloomsbury Academic, 2013.

Baudrillard, Jean. "Why Theory?" In *Hatred of Capitalism*, edited by Chriss Krauss and Sylvère Lotringer, 129–31. Los Angeles: Semiotext(e), 2001.

Benjamin, Walter. "The Work of Art in the Age of Its Technological Reproducibility." In *The Work of Art in the Age of Its Technological Reproducibility and Other Writings on Media*, edited by Michael W. Jennings, et al., translated by Edmund Jephcott, et al. Cambridge: Harvard University Press, 2008.

Bhabha, Homi. *The Location of Culture*. London: Routledge, 1994.

Butler, Judith. *The Psychic Life of Power: Theories in Subjection*. Stanford: Stanford University Press, 1997.

Canguilhem, Georges and Charles Ehresmann. "Editors' Notice." In Cavaillès, *On Logic and the Theory of Science*, translated by Robin Mackay and Knox Peden. New York: Urbanomic/Sequence Press, 2021.

Cavaillès, Jean. *On Logic and the Theory of Science*.

Cook, Alexander C. (ed). *Mao's Little Red Book: A Global History*. Cambridge: Cambridge University Press, 2014.

Davis, Oliver. *Jacques Rancière*. Cambridge: Polity Press, 2010.

de Man, Paul. *Aesthetic Ideology*. Minneapolis: University of Minnesota Press, 1996.

Derrida, Jacques. *Specters of Marx: The State of Debt, the Work of Mourning, and The New International*, translated by Peggy Kamuf. New York: Routledge, 1994.

Duroux, Yves. "A Philosophical Conjuncture: An Interview with Étienne Balibar and Yves Duroux." In *Concept and Form, Volume Two: Interviews and Essays on the* Cahiers pour l'Analyse, edited by Peter Hallward and Knox Peden. London: Verso, 2012.

Elliott, Gregory. *Althusser: The Detour of Theory*. Chicago: Haymarket Books, 2009.

Fardy, Jonathan. "Photographism in Althusser's Theory of Ideology: (Notes Toward a Non-Philosophical Investigation)." *Angelaki: Journal of the Theoretical Humanities*, Vol. 25, No. 5 (2021): 135–44.

Fardy, Jonathan. *The Real Is Radical: Marx after Laruelle*. London: Bloomsbury Academic, 2022.

Flusser, Vilém. *Towards a Philosophy of Photography*, translated by Anthony Mathews. London: Reaktion Books, 2012.

Freud, Sigmund. *The Interpretation of Dreams*, translated by James Strachey. London: Penguin, 1976.

Fried, Michael. *Art and Objecthood: Essays and Reviews*. Chicago: The University of Chicago Press, 1998.

Gane, Mike (ed). *Baudrillard Live: Selected Interviews*. London: Routledge, 1993.

Gane, Mike. *Jean Baudrillard: In Radical Uncertainty*. London: Pluto Press, 2000.

Garaudy, Roger. *Marxism in the Twentieth Century*, translated by René Hague. New York: Charles Scribner's Sons, 1970.

Greenberg, Clement. "Modernist Painting." In *Modern Art and Modernism: A Critical Anthology*, edited by Francis Frascina and Charles Harrison. New York: Routledge, 2019.

Hallward, Peter and Knox Peden (eds). *Concept and Form, Volume One: Key Texts from the* Cahiers pour l'Analyse. London: Verso, 2012.

Hallward, Peter and Knox Peden (eds). *Concept and Form, Volume Two: Interviews and Essays on the* Cahiers pour l'Analyse. London: Verso, 2012.

Hallward, Peter. "Introduction: Theoretical Training." In *Concept and Form, Volume One*.

Hartman, Geoffrey. *Saving the Text: Literature, Derrida, Philosophy*. Baltimore: The Johns Hopkins University Press, 1981.

James, Ian. "Review of *Introduction to Non-Marxism*." *Notre Dame Philosophical Reviews*, December 12, 2013. https://ndpr.nd.edu/reviews/introduction-to-non-marxism/.

James, Ian. *The New French Philosophy*. Cambridge: Polity Press, 2012.

Jay, Martin. *Downcast Eyes: The Denigration of Vision in Twentieth-Century French Thought*. Berkeley: University of California Press, 1994.

Judd, Donald. "Specific Objects." In *Art in Theory, 1900–200: An Anthology of Changing Ideas*, edited by Charles Harrison and Paul Wood. Malden: Blackwell Publishing, 2003.

Kofman, Sarah. *Camera Obscura: Of Ideology*, translated by Will Straw. Ithaca: Cornell University Press, 1999.

Kolozova, Katerina. *Capitalism's Holocaust of Animals: A Non-Marxist Critique of Capital, Philosophy, and Patriarchy*. London: Bloomsbury Academic, 2020.

Kolozova, Katerina. *Toward a Radical Metaphysics of Socialism: Marx and Laruelle*. Brooklyn: Punctum Books, 2015.

Labica, Georges. *Marxism and the Status of Philosophy*, translated by Kate Soper and Martin Ryle. Sussex: The Harvester Press, 1980.

Laruelle, François. *Introduction to Non-Marxism*, translated by Anthony Paul Smith. Minneapolis: Univocal Publishing, 2015.

Laruelle, François. *Photo-Fiction, a Non-standard Aesthetics*, translated by Drew S. Burk. Minneapolis: Univocal Publishing, 2012.

Laruelle, François. *The Concept of Non-photography*, translated by Robin Mackay. New York: Urbanomic/Sequence Press, 2012.

Laruelle, François. *Theory of Identities*, translated by Alyosha Edlebi. New York: Columbia University Press, 2016.

Lippard, Lucy. *Six Years: The Dematerialization of the Art Object from 1966–1972*. Berkeley: University of California Press, 2001.

Marx, Karl. *Capital, Vol. I*. In *Collected Works, Vol. 35*. New York: International Publishers, 2017.

Marx, Karl and Frederick Engels. "The German Ideology." In *Collected Works, Vol. 5, 1845–7*. New York: International Publishers, 2018.

Miller, Jacques-Alain. "Action of the Structure." In *Concept and Form: Volume One*.

Negri, Antonio. *Marx in Movement: Operaismo in Context*, translated by Ed Emery. Cambridge: Polity Press, 2022.

Nesbitt, Nick. *The Price of Slavery: Capitalism and Revolution in the Caribbean*. Charlottesville: University of Virginia Press, 2022.

Pang, Laikwan. *The Art of Cloning: Creative Production during China's Cultural Revolution*. London: Verso, 2010.

Peden, Knox. "'Autonomy, Therefore Necessity:' Jean Cavaillès's Contribution to a Theory of Science." In Cavaillès, *On Logic and the Theory of Science*.

Peden, Knox. *Spinoza Contra Phenomenology: French Rationalism from Cavaillès to Deleuze*. Stanford: Stanford University Press, 2014.

Rancière, Jacques. *Althusser's Lesson*, translated by Emiliano Battista. London: Bloomsbury Academic, 2011.

Rancière, Jacques. *Proletarian Nights: The Workers' Dream in Nineteenth-Century France*, translated by John Drury. New York: Verso, 2012.

Redfield, Marc. *Theory at Yale: The Strange Case of Deconstruction in America*. Brooklyn: Fordham University Press, 2015.

Ross, Kristin. "Historicizing Untimeliness." In *Jacques Rancière: History, Politics, Aesthetics*, edited by Gabriel Rockhill and Philip Watts. Durham: Duke University Press, 2009.

Sohn-Rethel, Alfred. *Intellectual and Manual Labor*, translated by Martin Sohn-Rethel. Leiden: Brill, 2021.

Sotiris, Panagiotis. *A Philosophy for Communism: Rethinking Althusser*. Chicago: Haymarket Books, 2021.

Thompson, E. P. *The Making of the English Working Class*. New York: Vintage, 1966.

Thompson, E. P. *The Poverty of Theory*. London: Monthly Review Press, 2008.

Tronti, Mario. *Workers and Capital*, translated by David Broder. New York: Verso, 2019.

Tse-Tung, Mao. "On Practice." In *Selected Works of Mao Tse-Tung: Volume I*. Peking: Foreign Language Press, 1965.

Tse-Tung, Mao. *On the Correct Handling of Contradictions among the People*. Peking: Foreign Language Press, 1966.

Ulmer, Gregory. "The Object of Post-Criticism." In *The Anti-Aesthetic: Essays on Postmodern Culture*, edited by Hal Foster. Port Townsend: Bay Press, 1983.

Wolin, Richard. *The Politics of Being: The Political Thought of Martin Heidegger*. New York: Columbia University Press, 1990.

Wolin, Richard. *The Wind from the East: French Intellectuals, the Cultural Revolution, and the Legacy of the 1960s*. Princeton: Princeton University Press, 2017.

Wright, Steve. *Storming Heaven: Class Composition and Struggle in Italian Autonomous Marxism*. London: Pluto Press, 2017.

Index

A
aesthetics, Althusserian 114, 115, 138, 139
   bourgeois 43
   ideology of 136, 137
   minimalist 97–8
   modernist 97, 98, 137
   non-standard 134, 136
affect 82–4
agency of theory 19, 28, 113, 149
Althusserianism 2, 4, 63–6, 68, 150
Althusser's Lesson (Rancière) 4, 57, 65–6
anti-humanism 22, 29, 30, 42, 67
anti-mimetic 96–7, 109, 134, 145
Armstrong, Philip 126–7
Autonomous Marxism 4, 76–8, 80, 85
axiomatic 19, 23, 30, 119, 134–5, 14

B
Bachelard, Gaston 12
Badiou, Alain 13, 36, 41–3, 63, 150
Balestrini, Nanni 82–3
banal strategy 110
Bargu, Banu 114
Benjamin, Walter 37, 127–8
Butler, Judith 114

C
cadre 18–19, 31, 37, 45, 65
Cahiers pour l'Analyse 15
Cailloux 74–6
Canguilhem, Georges 12
Capital (Marx) 8, 20, 23–4, 85, 127, 140
Cavaillès, Jean 3, 7, 11, 13, 16, 19, 23
class struggle 27, 28, 30, 35, 36, 44–5, 47–8, 64, 75, 79, 113, 134, 140

commodity fetishism 8–10, 29, 101, 149
communism 37, 41, 43, 72, 107–9
Communist Manifesto, The (Marx and Engels) 85, 108
Concept of Non-Photography, The (Laruelle) 119
consciousness 2–3, 5, 8–10, 13, 16, 29, 31, 46, 51, 94, 110–11, 114, 149, 150, 153
Correct Handling of Contradictions Among the People, On the (Zedong) 14
co-research 76–7, 79–81, 85
cult of personality 38–41, 150
Cultural Revolution 37–42
"Cultural Revolution, On" (Althusser) 33–4
curvature 102–4

D
Dagoreau 75
Davis, Oliver 69–71, 76
de Man, Paul 5, 139, 140, 152
de-Stalinization 22, 149
descriptive theory 47–9, 55
determination-in-the-last instance 59, 120, 134–5, 145
de Tracy, Destutt 7
division of labor 64–5, 68, 71, 77, 81, 84, 137, 150–1
Duroux, Yves 16

E
Ehresmann, Charles 12
Elliot, Gregory 19
emancipated spectator 73–5
empiricism 13, 87, 149
   as ideology 17–8, 24

Index

empirical proletarians 3, 70–4, 87
epistemology 3, 21, 27, 32, 110, 120, 139, 149
Essays in Self-Criticism (Althusser) 35
Estes, Richard 94
Evans, Walker 95
exchange 9, 10, 17, 32, 132–3

F
Fardy, Jonathan 147n.30
Fatal Strategies (Baudrillard) 95–6, 107
fatal strategy 102, 104, 110
Flusser, Vilém 121–2, 129
Forget Foucault (Baudrillard) 96
For Marx (Althusser) 3, 21, 24, 115, 132
Foucault, Michel 13, 31, 73, 96, 144
French Communist Party 13, 15, 29, 42, 66, 68
Freud, Sigmund 52–3
Fried, Michael 98

G
Gane, Mike 94
Garaudy, Roger 29, 42
German Ideology, The (Marx and Engels) 7–8, 50
Gilland, J. -P. 71–3, 76
Glas (Derrida) 96–9, 101
Greenberg, Clement 97

H
Hallward, Peter 15
Hartman, Geoffrey 99
How to be a Marxist in Philosophy (Althusser) 114
Hyperreal 94–5, 102–4, 106

I
iconophobia 134, 143
ideological critique 2, 94, 100, 109
ideological state apparatuses 3, 46, 49, 53, 127–8

immanence 38
in-struggle 133
of the photo 124–5, 133
of the real 125
Intelligence of Evil, The (Baudrillard) 102
interpellation 1, 2, 45, 54, 55, 56, 58, 114–15, 126, 150, 153
Baudrillard's critique 111
Rancière's critique 65
Laruelle's critique 126
Introduction to Non-Marxism (Laruelle) 131, 143

J
James, Ian 65, 143–4
Judd, Donald 98

K
Khrushchev, Nikita 14, 22, 39
Kofman, Sarah 8
Kolozova, Katerina 145
Kosuth, Joseph 99

L
Labica, Georges 7
Lenin and Philosophy (Althusser) 54, 113, 140
Lenin, Vladimir 34, 35, 48
"Letter on Art" (Althusser) 137
Levine, Sherrie 94–5
Lippard, Lucy 99
"Logical Revolts" (Rancière) 70, 76, 87, 150
Lukács, Georg 9, 51, 99, 149

M
Mao 14, 34, 35–7, 42, 44, 83, 150
as signifier 38–9, 41, 45
Maoism 4, 34, 43, 150
aesthetics of, 36, 41–2, 150
in China 36, 37
in France 36, 37, 42, 69, 150

Marxism-humanism 21, 24, 27, 67, 68
Leninism 14, 27, 34, 35, 44, 45, 63, 65, 67, 150
Miller, Jacques-Alain 30–2, 42

N
Nesbitt, Nick 9
non-philosophy 2, 119, 120, 132, 134, 135, 141–6
non-photography 119, 123, 125, 134

O
object of knowledge 11, 21, 24, 45, 129, 130, 141, 143, 146
objectality 98, 99, 100, 101, 104, 109, 115, 153
occularcentrism 144
Logic and the Theory of Science, On (Cavaillès) 10–11
On Practice (Zedong) 35

P
Pang, Laikwan 37–9, 42, 150
Peden, Knox 10–13, 23–4
Philosophical Decision 125, 131, 138, 140–1, 143, 145, 152
Philosophy and the Spontaneous Philosophy of the Scientists (Althusser) 34
philosophy as capital 131
of the concept 3, 10, 13, 29, 149
photo-fiction 134–5, 152
Photo-Fiction, a Non-Standard Aesthetics (Laruelle) 134–5, 152
photographism 5, 119, 120, 125, 128–9, 131
photographocentric 121–2, 126–7, 131, 134, 135–6, 143, 152
post-criticism 5, 96–9, 145, 151
postmodernism 97–8, 105
principle of sufficient philosophy 119
Proletarian Nights (Rancière) 4, 64, 69–72, 74–6, 85–7

R
rationalism 11
Reading Capital (Althusser) 2–3, 14, 17, 23–4, 30, 111, 113, 127–9
Redfield, Marc 96
refusal 4, 76, 82, 87
reification 9
"Reply to John Lewis" (Althusser) 27
repressive state apparatus 48–9
Rosenquist, James 101
Ross, Kristin 72, 73

S
Saint-Simonians 75–6
science in Althusser 15, 18, 19–21, 23–4, 28, 33, 45, 50, 64–8, 111, 113, 146
Cavaillès 10–12, 16, 31
Laruelle 131, 140–4, 146, 152
Mao 45, 78
Marxism 18, 19, 22, 79, 87, 150–1
Shadow of the Silent Majorities, In the (Baudrillard) 9, 103
simulacrum 94–5, 103, 105–7, 131
simulation 93, 94, 103, 105, 123
Simulations (Baudrillard) 35, 103
Sohn-Rethel, Alfred 10, 17
Sotiris, Panagiotis 22
specter in Baudrillard 105, 109–10, 115
Specters of Marx (Derrida) 107–8
Spinozism 11–13, 21
spirit in Baudrillard 109–11, 151
in Derrida 107–8
state form 53–4, 57, 62n.61
Stella, Frank 97
structuralism 31–2
structured results 31
structuring processes 16, 18, 24, 30, 81
subject of consciousness 110–11
critique 17, 109–10, 151
exchange 17
history 28, 133

ideology 115
individual 130, 131
knowledge 1, 112
Maoism 36
militancy 44
science 23
struggle 133
theory 3, 4, 19, 88
the real 131
truth 100
subjection 3, 45, 46, 49, 53, 56, 58, 65, 115, 130-1, 134, 146
superstructure 34, 46-7, 55, 120
System of Objects, The (Baudrillard) 99, 101

T
theatre 55, 67, 114, 115, 126
theoreticism 35, 45, 59, 87
theory form 56-7
Theory of Identities (Laruelle) 141, 143
Theory of the Subject (Badiou) 43-4
the real in Althusser 17-18, 21, 129-30, 138

Baudrillard 93-4, 95, 100, 102-8
Cavaillès 11
Laruelle 59, 119-21, 123, 125, 131-2, 134-6, 142, 144-6, 152
Thompson, E. P. 29, 84
Tronti, Mario 78-9, 81-2
Twentieth Congress of CPSU 14, 22, 40, 44

U
Ulmer, Gregory 5, 96-9, 145, 151

V
Véret, Désirée 75-6
Violet, Alphonse 74

W
"Why Theory?" (Baudrillard) 102
Wolin, Richard 36-7, 150
workerism 78-9, 151
workers against work 4, 74, 81
working class 22, 47, 49, 69-70, 72, 74, 76-9, 81-2, 84, 87-88, 150-1
Wright, Steve 80

www.ingramcontent.com/pod-product-compliance
Lightning Source LLC
Chambersburg PA
CBHW052128300426
44116CB00010B/1813